Becoming an Insightful Leader
Charting Your Course to Purposeful Success

David Spitulnik

2/26/20

RALPH —

KEEP ON BECOMING.

KEEP ON LEADING.

DAVID

Becoming an Insightful Leader
Copyright ©2018 David Spitulnik

ISBN 978-1506-906-75-1 PBK
ISBN 978-1506-906-76-8 EBK

LCCN 2018952680

July 2018

Published and Distributed by
First Edition Design Publishing, Inc.
P.O. Box 20217, Sarasota, FL 34276-3217
www.firsteditiondesignpublishing.com

Cover Design: Hutchinson Associates, Inc.

Introduction

"It is important for people to understand that they not only do things right but are doing the right thing."

Helena Stelnicki, Owner of Stelnicki Partners

Obviously, many books out there have been written about leadership. I noticed that as I absorbed them through the years, I started to take on many of the leadership qualities mentioned as well. What I was fascinated to discover was I just wasn't one type of leader. I would find myself shifting gears to become a *different type of leader* based on what the environment threw at me in that moment.

I thought I was very atypical. Then I started talking to many of the people you'll see quoted in this book – *and as it turned out, they were functioning in the same manner too!* You couldn't define them nice and neatly within one type of "leader checkbox." These leaders frequently found themselves changing their styles all the time based on their given situation.

That's when I realized what I was and what these many other people were... An **Insightful Leader.**

Rather than applying one leadership style to all situations across the board, all Insightful Leaders are a *composite entity* who operates in a world that is situationally dependent. They are always in a state of shifting, pivoting and adapting. They understand what is needed at that point in time to address both the issues that they're facing outwardly as well as what is happening with the team.

In one of the chapters in this book, we'll talk about how you can instruct someone to "take the hill" as a leader, meaning that that individual will need to follow a clear direction you've given them.

Can you do that every single day? No. Because on another day, that person may not be able to operate as independently as the day before and may require extra help from the insight you have to attack the situation at hand. That person may have a great deal of technical skill but still needs someone next to him, watching to ensure he's going about a task in the right way.

Remember, we're just talking about *one* member of the team too. Every individual member of the team may need something different in that moment from you in order to do their part and get the task done.

At face value, this may seem overwhelming in its complexity – *"Wait. In order to be an Insightful Leader...I have to be a different leader for every type of situation?"* Yes. However, if we deconstruct the elements of the situation, we can begin to make it easier to address.

To start, there are three major environment types: The **Stable Environment**, the **High Growth Environment** that is rapidly evolving and the **Environment In Crisis.** These environments are quite different from one another, but you'll know before very long exactly which one you're standing in.

Secondly, there is the internal environment that pertains to **your team.** Beyond what each individual is going through (personally and professionally), what does the team need from you and from the company to be successful? What are their general emotions right now and what does that team bring in terms of an overall skill set to move the company forward?

How can you help create a setting that is conducive to that group's skill set?

Third, don't forget that you have to look in the mirror and **know thyself**, meaning that as you're striving to be in touch with the atmosphere and emotions of your people, it's vital to have self-awareness of your own presence, messages you're putting out there and how you're being perceived.

As you strive to address these moving parts, make sure you have some perspective about the process.

> ### *Reaching the destination as an Insightful Leader does not happen overnight. It is a journey.*

I'd also suggest that you probably won't say, *"Well, I did A, B and C, so I'm an Insightful Leader now!"* The realization of this moment is more likely to occur in reflection over the journey you've made.

That's certainly what happened to me. When I reflect back on periods of my life, I can see the seeds of being an Insightful Leader that I couldn't at the time.

In the Boy Scouts, I was elected to be a Senior Patrol Leader of a provisional troop for one week at camp and ultimately helped that troop win a camp-wide competition. This was, according to the staff, the first time that a provisional troop had ever won. It happened because I was able to **recognize which people performed particular tasks the very best and help each person understand their role in achieving the team's goal.**

In college, when I was asked to be Captain of the track team, we'd not won a meet in the previous three years. Our new coach, who had just taken charge, felt that I was someone who was in constant communication with the team and a person they could feel comfortable talking to. I didn't think of myself as an Insightful Leader at the time but I did come to see that being a leader was as much about **understanding the emotions of the team and environ-**

ment that the team was operating in – and that both could change rapidly.

In the workplace, you can be thrown into a variety of environments and one of my early positions was the first time I truly understood the importance of culture. I was beginning to lead not only people from the U.S. but also leading international teams. People from the U.S. needed to be led in a certain way but people from different countries needed to be led in another way at times. Over time, as I was setting up deals and partnerships internationally, while I knew a lot about business, I didn't always understand how these cultures worked and interacted with each other. Once I gained more of that insight and put aside my preconceived notions on how to lead and interact with others, I built relationships with a lot more common sense in tow. I made a **conscious effort to understand the person I was dealing with in order to get the highest return from what they were doing.** This would prove to be an ever-continuing evolution.

"Insight is the power of acute observation, deduction, penetration, discernment and perception."

Pearl Zhu "Future of CIO" Blog

The Three "I's"

The experiences in life that have shaped my formation as an Insightful Leader relate directly to the three essential "I's" that Pearl Zhu, writer of the "Future of CIO" Blog, has identified.

The Insightful Leader must always possess these qualities, no matter how much the environment they're in changes.

> **Intelligence** – Beyond being able to understand and encapsulate other things that people have been doing before, intelligence is also

about being smart enough to understand what solution best fits with the environment you're currently facing. How does that idea fit with understanding those around you and what they bring to you at this point in time? One more element within intelligence is having the presence of mind to know your strongest qualities and skills while recognizing that you need help with other crucial areas.

Inclusion – Bringing to bear all the resources you have, full inclusion of team members will often help you understand what you have and don't have for a given challenge. It's about embracing differences because, after all, someone can be different, but you don't want to exclude them just because they're different. Such variety can be an invaluable asset.

Influence – You have the emotional and intellectual wherewithal to be effective at what you do and because of what you know. Influence comes from who you know and *who your connections know*. That involves asking for help when you need it. For instance, let's say you want to know someone who has XYX skill set and you're not ashamed to say, *"I don't know that kind of person."* But you also will immediately follow that thought with, *"...but I can find somebody who does."* On many occasions, this influence is built from mutual referral – you refer someone to a strategic partner because that strategic partner refers people to you. So you'll ask them for help on something because they're going to ask you for help on something. If they help you address the problem on the table, they'll rise to the top of the referral list.

This pyramid of Intelligence-Inclusion-Influence, along with different leadership styles, all work together to form the Insightful Leader.

So where do we go from here together?

The purpose of this book is to help you navigate this wonderful journey to being an Insightful Leader. My hope is that throughout each chapter, you'll take a look in the mirror and understand your place along the path to better leadership. There are peaks and valleys in this journey to come, but simply making the choice to learn about areas for improvement is a monumental first step. Just remember that as much as you'll learn to adapt to different environments, people and challenges, there are some elements that you should never want to change, such as your integrity.

As I share some of the personal and professional stories from my life that have helped build my leadership qualities, I encourage you to think about the experiences in your own life and realize that you're not the first person who has gone through this exercise.

To maximize your understanding, at the end of each chapter, I've included three crucial areas that you won't want to skip over:

Takeaways that highlight the primary lessons of the chapter to remember

Exercises that you should give some careful thought to and answer

Decision Matrix Questions that will help you customize a path forward that will ultimately enhance how you lead today as well as tomorrow

Ready to go? *Let's start on the path together toward Becoming an Insightful Leader.*

1

If I Had Known Then...

"I was an organizer from an early age. An important element of many of these activities revolved around fairness to all involved."

Steve Haggerty, President of Haggerty Consulting and Mayor of Evanston, Illinois

My first real experience as a leader came when I was elected the captain of my high school's soccer team. It wasn't a position that I actively sought, but I was elated nonetheless when this happened.

Then, as I began to realize what was expected of me, both by my teammates as well as our coach, I came to a realization: I might be in over my head! However, as the season wore on and I got used to the role, I realized that I could live up to everyone's expectations, including my own, and still have a good time playing the game.

At the time, it was easy to think that my captainship was all the result of some popularity contest. Yet, looking back, I now realize that I was elected as captain because those around me wanted something from me – *they were looking for my advice and counsel about how to raise their game.*

So, before I knew that leadership was a journey, you could say I was already on the train to my destination and starting to learn.

The Election – Based On Popularity or Results?

As I stop and look back on this experience, there are quite a few points worth noting. First and foremost, I learned a lot in the process of being elected to a leadership position. What I didn't know then that I do know now is that it is very different to be *elected* versus being *appointed or promoted* into a position.

My election came from two things much bigger than popularity:

➢ An **expectation** on the part of those around me about what I was going to do with and for them.

➢ A **mission** they believed I could help them accomplish - winning soccer games and having fun doing it. A significant part of this mission was to be the on-field leader of the team and to represent the team when there was an issue with something that the referees did.

As I also came to realize, my new role dealt with things that happened away from the field too. I was called on to help other members of the team address issues that had nothing at all to do with soccer. Sometimes they were school-related. Other times, my teammates just wanted someone to listen to them.

Plus, while the team elected me, there were also expectations that came from our soccer coach. This was my first experience of being a *member* of a team and having an entirely separate set of expectations as a result of being a *team leader.* I had to learn to organize, prioritize and respond to these expectations in different ways which was dependent on the source; whether from my peers or from more senior people.

> **"If you want to remember it and sell
> the concepts to others,
> they need to be written down."**
> Mark Shapiro, a former senior leader at The
> Quaker Oats Company and now a Vistage Chair.

Understanding the Rules

Two things stand out in my mind from the day of the soccer election: One was the intense sense of pride from the recognition of my peers. The other was the intense sense of disbelief when my coach handed me the then-current set of rules for high school soccer – because, again, part of the role of captain was to be the team's on-field advocate.

When you think about it, that's a lot on the plate of a high school senior. You've got academics. You've got college applications. You're playing a varsity sport. And of course, whenever you can, you're simply trying to enjoy your last year of high school.

On top of that, now you have to keep current on soccer rules not only to be a better player but also be the advocate when you feel the referees are wrong? Let's just say it can be quite scary as well as fascinating.

Adaptive Leadership

When I was elected team captain, it didn't take long for me to understand that I had to take the time to learn what the rest of the team, both as a group and as individuals, wanted from me. What motivated them? Why did they select me? What were their expectations of me if I wanted to be an effective leader for them?

In retrospect, it was in this role that I first learned about **adaptive leadership,** which is the notion that a good leader needs to understand:

> ➤ What makes each member of their team tick?

- The role that the team members want the leader to play.
- The way that each team member needs to be motivated to get his or her duties accomplished.

When our team made the playoffs for the first time in several years, I knew that there was *something* there that had an influence. I now believe that this Adaptive Leadership style on my part was a key element of our team's success.

> *"I spent a lot of time asking people how they did their jobs and what they thought that they needed to be able to do them better."*
> Martin Swarbrick, former CEO of Bison Gear & Engineering

The De Facto Leader

One of the reasons why people are elected to these leadership roles, beyond the element of popularity, is the notion that team members are looking for someone to listen to them while helping them get their job done and grow. In many organizations, there are the people who are elected and or named in the leadership positions. Then there are the people who are *actually leading* or the **De Facto Leaders**. These are the people who, independent of their actual title, are looked to for counsel on how to make things work and how to get things done.

I learned another valuable lesson in leadership four years later, once again in athletics, when I was named captain of the track team during my senior year in college.

Our new coach walked into a situation where we had not won a meet in several years. When it became apparent to him that other members of the team were coming to me for counsel, he turned to me for assistance. He wanted someone who understood that leaders put the team first and were willing to stay engaged through the disappointment of losing. He also wanted someone who was willing to lead, whether or not they had the official title of captain.

This notion is also similar to the notion of centers of influence as compared to centers of authority. **It is critical that we understand what others see in us and expect from us in order to chart our course to purposeful success.**

What I Do Know Now...

While these leadership roles were somewhat unique, there are many similarities to leadership roles in corporate, not-for-profit and other group and association settings. You often have to seek leadership roles – they don't usually just fall into your lap. It's also about understanding the people with whom you are working and the needs and expectations of all of your constituencies.

In retrospect, the early lessons from my athletic experiences in school have served as a sound foundation for leadership experiences that I've had later on in life, both when I was elected as well as when I was promoted into the position.

A team, or an organization, is positioned for success when its leaders are ready to provide advice and counsel, within reason, for situations that directly have to do with "the game" and those that have to do with what is going on in each team member's life. It doesn't mean that the leader has to be an all-knowing therapist. Rather, the leader is there to help the members of the team find the resources for other issues that they are facing.

Mike Petersen
CEO
Petersen Aluminum Corporation

Mike represents his family's second generation of leadership at Petersen Aluminum Corp., a $150 million firm that manufactures metal applications for architectural and structural roofing as well as wall paneling. Mike knew his father wanted him to go into the family business from the moment the company was founded in 1965, when Mike was just 10 years old. Today, from the company's headquarters in the Chicago metropolitan area, Mike leads a management team that has averaged 34 years of employment.

If I had to advise anyone aspiring to be a leader, there are three things I'd strongly suggest:

Don't be afraid to take risks.

Yes, think through the situation as well as you can, but don't be afraid to make mistakes – if you make them, learn from them. It's about adjusting from those mistakes so that you have a positive takeaway.

When you get an opportunity handed to you, don't get so set in your ways that you miss it. Think of what that opportunity might do for you. When a company approached my father with the chance to fabricate in a new and more cost-effective manner, he didn't hesitate and jumped on it. Or when I told my father that we could become as big a company by manufacturing steel instead of aluminum, he was on board with that direction too.

Study and learn from the marketing plan of your competitors. In your critical analysis, how are your competitors going to market? What can you learn from that? It can't hurt to have curiosity about a lot of other businesses – for example, our industry isn't known for social media marketing, but our company capitalized on it early on. When it comes down to it, we need to market to architects and building developers who are visual thinkers, even if they're two or three steps away from ordering our product.

TAKEAWAYS

Consequently, the conclusions from these early leadership experiences include:

* ❖ **Walk the talk** – it is about being genuine as a leader.

* ❖ **Live the values** – whatever the organization, you're always on display as the leader, whether on the field or in a meeting.

* ❖ **Work with others to make them better** – by seeking to raise each individual's game, you are raising the entire team's game. I am reminded of the famous quote *"Winning isn't everything. It's the only thing."* I would suggest that it be modified to *"Winning isn't everything – it's the only thing besides growing while you are doing it."*

* ❖ **Understand what is out of bounds** – as sports typically have a well-defined set of rules and regulations, this is typically one of the best places to begin this learning exercise. However, it is also important to understand when there are different interpretations of the rules so that you can help lead your team through the grey areas.

* ❖ **Understand that even if you don't have the title, you may be playing the role** – if you have what it takes to lead, people will look to you to do so, independent of whether you have been appointed or elected to the role.

* ❖ **Listen, watch and learn** – this applies to all people and situations you encounter. One hopes that most of these learning opportunities will involve things to do. However, be open to learning what *not* to do too.

EXERCISES

I have been told for as long as I can remember that the best way *"to learn it is to live it."* Therefore, while we will do our best to make the ideas clear, we will also provide exercises in each chapter to assist you in better understanding the concepts discussed.

We started off by talking about the role of the elected leader, how to better understand what goes into being elected to the position as well as understanding how and why you are - or are not – suited for the role.

The first exercise deals with understanding how a role is defined and then whether or not you have what it would take to accomplish the role.

❖ Describe an organization (a team or board) you are part of where the leader is elected.

❖ Write the job description for the attributes of the leader other than the function specific attributes of the board/team.

❖ Perform a self-assessment of which attributes you have and which you don't have.

❖ Of those attributes, which are most critical and why?

Another of the major elements of the chapter dealt with the notion of those who hold power not because of their title, but because of *who they are.* There are some who have power in an organization because they have the title and others who hold power because they control access to some valuable asset, be it specific information or some physical asset. The De Facto Leader, however, typically has neither. Rather they are the *informal influence center.*

In the following, through drawing of actual and de facto organization charts, the goal is to help to understand how these control structures can coexist. Through understanding the informal structure, how can the elected/appointed leaders make the organization stronger?

The De Facto Leader

❖ Pick an organization you are part of or lead.

❖ Draw the official organization chart of that organization.

❖ Research who people turn to for help or information – people who are *not* at the top of their groups.

❖ Define the different attributes of the official structure and the de facto structure.

❖ What can be learned? How can the de facto structure be used by the appointed/ elected leaders to further the mission of the organization?

DECISION MATRIX QUESTIONS

❖ Why am I being *selected* to lead?

❖ Why am I being *elected* to lead?

❖ Am I the formal leader (elected/appointed) or the De Facto Leader (one to whom decisions are deferred)?

❖ What are the areas that people seek my counsel in?

❖ Do I understand the rules, both formal and informal, for leading the organization?

2

What Do You Want To Be When You Grow Up?

"It is critical to understand what vacuum you are filling."

Stuart Baum, President, Larger Pond Marketing

"What do you want to be when you grow up?"

It's one of the questions that we're often asked as young children. When we're young, it's more of game or fantasy. However, as we get older, it becomes more of a real question.

For most of us, the end of college (and for some, the end of high school) represents a time when we have to start thinking in earnest about what we want to do with the rest of our lives. While it's necessary to complete an application to be admitted to college, building a resume is a new experience. Unlike the college application, there isn't a set of guidelines as to how the resume should be constructed. Typically, if you speak with three career counselors, you'll get at least four or five opinions about what makes a good resume. That said, the key to it all is the **Career Objective.**

When I was going through this exercise myself toward the end of my college experience, I realized that there were many ways of attacking the Career Objective. I could be like one of my classmates, whose objective was very specific: He wanted to be head of Proctor and Gamble. Another one of my classmates also had specific (though not really career-oriented) statements such as how he wanted to be in a position where he could see the world – which was interesting, but not very helpful.

As I began thinking about who I was and who I wanted to be, I realized that being in a position to influence and perhaps even drive an organization was my objective. I understood that this probably would not happen overnight, but rather would come as a result of being recognized as someone who thought about how to provide good, if not great, answers to questions. I'd also strive to be seen as someone who could be relied upon to ask good, if not great, questions.

With all of this in mind, my objective was:

"To be in a position where my opinions are requested and respected."

I'll admit that this was not met with a great deal of support from the career counselors that I was working with. However, I stuck to my guns and continued to use it for several years.

A few years ago, it was suggested to me that I stopped one short of where I really wanted to be. That is, my true objective was:

"To be in a position where my opinions are requested, respected and acted on."

Now, it is critical to note that my opinions aren't always acted on, but at least being in the conversation is key. To quote from the hit musical *Hamilton*, I not only wanted to be *"in the room where it happens."* I also wanted to have an active role in the discussion.

> ***"For all private businesses, the scorecard is a continuum, not just 12 months."***
> Richard Nathan, President, RTC

The Career Objective as Part of the Journey

As stated earlier, while I was being asked to take on leadership roles, it was really not yet apparent to me how these roles supported my long-term ambitions. Looking back, I can see that the leadership foundation was being laid but I had no idea what the final structure was going to look like. In fact, the building is still in process.

In retrospect, I don't remember ever really having a discussion with anyone about how career planning was an important part of life planning – even though for many years, my jobs and career would consume most of my waking hours. I believe that I was fortunate that my advisors grudgingly gave me the latitude to develop such a non-specific and aspirational statement. Again, it gave me something to strive for, but not a specific endpoint where I could say that I was done.

This "career objective" as part of the resume seems to have lost favor. However, in working as a coach and mentor for both new and established leaders, the starting point of the discussion is to define where individuals want to be at specific points in their careers, both short and long term.

This notion of identifying the objective or objectives and then the paths to get there is relevant for career, life and even business planning.

Equally as important is spending the time necessary to develop the criteria you will use to assess progress, actually assessing the progress and, as necessary, making changes to get you back on track or to change the objectives.

How Will We Know When We Get There?

While I had a general, intellectual understanding of what it was that I sought, I did not really understand the practicalities of what I was asking for until the mid-point of my time with Motorola. I was asked by the leader of one of the largest teams to join his organization with the "official" title of Director, Business Development.

He went on to say, however, that my unofficial title would be to serve as director of "What do you think about that?"

While I understood this industry, I had not worked in this particular business segment, so I was coming in without the biases that many of those who had been there for a long time had. In this role, I would participate in most meetings with him and if something came up that he wanted an opinion on, I would be the person he would turn to. A non-traditional role, to say the least.

More critically, however, was how far out of the normal process the leader who asked me to take on the role was moving. He understood that in order to truly move the organization forward, he wanted someone who was not afraid to question and suggest paths that were outside of the accepted norms in his business. He truly had the insight that, in order to continue moving the business forward, he needed to make fundamental changes that were not in the normal course.

He challenged me to take on a new and different role, yet what he was really asking me to do was to take a step out of not only my comfort zone, but also the *organization's* traditional comfort zone.

I didn't realize this at the time, but in hindsight, this has helped me to drive others outside of their comfort zones so that they too can drive the organization forward.

Being Part of the Leadership Team vs. Being an Insightful Leader

Let's pause for a moment, though, to ask a question:

> **While being "in the room where it happens" may mean that you are part of the leadership team, does that make you an Insightful Leader?**

As I was being asked on a more frequent basis to participate as a member of leadership teams, I also began to better understand the truly broad array of leadership types and styles.

In the course of interviewing people for this book, one of the observations made was that truly Insightful Leaders don't talk about the fact that they are insightful leaders.

These leaders frequently noted that one of the attributes of insightful leadership was humility and therefore, in order to be a truly insightful AND great leader, one needs to BE it. Not just talk about it.

While Insightful Leaders usually don't refer to themselves with these characteristics, they usually do include these characteristics as part of what they hope to become. Furthermore, they often also talk about these traits as good success markers for leaders.

Is being an Insightful Leader part of who you are or who you want to become? Is it understood that just because you get there once, you won't necessarily stay there forever? With this in mind, how then do you become and remain an Insightful Leader?

Revisiting the Objectives

Remember my college classmate mentioned at the beginning at this chapter who wanted to be CEO at Proctor & Gamble? Well, he did wind up spending a few years there, but then he moved on after his first position. Why? He realized that the key for him was about the power of markets and understanding what consumers want. He has moved through a variety of industries, but all the while, he's remained true to the notion underlying his original Career

Objective: As a result, he is now Chief Insights and Innovation Officer for a consumer-oriented business.

How about my other classmate who wanted to see the world? He's been able to do so and he's worked in a number of different industries doing strategy and market development. In every case, he was willing to go almost anywhere. His understanding of how different cultures drive businesses in different ways has continued to develop. His count of countries visited is now in the high double digits and growing.

When we started, I am not sure that any of us could have articulated exactly why our original objective made sense. In hindsight, each of them has made sense and have helped drive our individual journeys.

Inga Carus
Chairman
Carus Group, Inc.

Inga leads Carus Group, Inc., a 102-year-old company that manufactures products responsible for cleaning aspects of the environment such as water, air and groundwater. As a very active Chairman, she has been focused on growth initiatives for the business related to mergers and acquisitions as well as new product development. Inga represents her family's third generation of leadership at Carus Group.

Did I know exactly what I wanted to be when I grew up? Well, if you would've told me that a former Chemist would ultimately be a business leader, I never would have believed it. On one hand, I always wanted to become a leader long before I actually was one. After all, even as a kid, I was particularly bossy! Yet, when I entered college, one thing I also knew is that I had no interest in going into business. I had heard about business every night during my childhood and thought it was boring.

So what changed my mind and opened my eyes to business? After finishing college with a Chemistry degree and doing professional work as a Chemist for three years, I started to see the value of doing something new and potentially adding value to the world. I truly enjoyed interacting with customers. Because I'm a people-focused person, I began to get interested in that aspect of business and realized that my skills would be well used. Having been exposed to something unique in a business environment, I decided to pursue an MBA from the University of Chicago. I then worked in a sales management capacity for a company for five years, including a stint overseas.

It proves how funny life can work out because here I am, years later, working in business and loving it. In fact, it's the only area I feel I could be good at too. I found this special place in my life by remembering to be true to myself, genuinely listening to others and viewing the process of learning different elements of business as a very fun and enjoyable experience.

TAKEAWAYS

❖ One first has to want to become a leader before one can become an Insightful Leader.

❖ Part of being a leader is wanting to be an active participant *"in the room where it happens."*

❖ As with any goal, one needs to have a set of defined metrics so that one can assess progress.

❖ Build a set of both long and short-term targets for yourself relative to your leadership journey.

❖ In order to grow as a leader, you must understand your comfort zone.

EXERCISES

As stated previously, if you want to learn it, then you have to *live* it.

While we may not need to define a Career Objective for our resume anymore, one needs to develop a plan to become and grow as a leader in general and an Insightful Leader specifically.

In this exercise:

❖ Define what YOUR leadership goals encompass.

❖ Be sure to define short-term and long-term goals as well as time-bound metrics to measure your progress along the way.

❖ To be clear, are these goals just about business or do they encompass other areas of your life as well?

❖ With the goal set in hand, now lay out why these are important and, for each time frame, what is the priority order of each goal articulated.

DECISION MATRIX QUESTIONS

❖ Do I understand my short- and long-term leadership objectives?

❖ Do I understand what the normal boundaries are for growing as a leader in my organization and are these boundaries acceptable to me?

3

From Manager to Leader

"Do what others choose not to do.
Presence has meaning and someone has
to care that you are there."

Matt Feldman, President and CEO, Federal Home Loan Bank of Chicago

I'm not sure when my eyes were opened to the notion that *managing* was different than *leading*. I have long believed that the two are different. However, it is apparent to me, that for some, there really is no difference at all.

With the help of those that I have been fortunate enough to interview, it is becoming clearer that managing is one step on the road to becoming an Insightful Leader.

From my perspective, managers are often those who lead by giving their teams specific directions on all elements of what needs to get done. They provide not only the goal, but also step-by-step instructions for how to get there. On the other hand, those who have moved beyond management alone into management *and* leadership, **discuss the goal**. And then, they get out of the way to allow the team and its members to determine the best way to reach the goal.

Let's take a step back for a moment and look at the definitions of managing and leading.

> ➤ A **manager** is a person who is responsible for *controlling or administering* all or part of a company or similar organization.
> ➤ A **leader**, on the other hand, is the one in charge – the person who *convinces* other people to follow.
> ➤ A great manager moves the team to action.
> ➤ A great leader inspires confidence in other people and moves them to action.

Let's Take a Look at the Journey

For many, the career path in a single organization starts with doing. In these roles, you have a set of tasks that you are responsible for. You take inputs from others, upon which you bend, fold and manipulate whatever you have been handed and then move it on to the next person in line.

After some time, if you are good at what you do, appear to have some skills at working with and engaging with others and, happen to be in the right place at the right time, you may be asked to manage the team (note that some may be asked to take on the role independent of how good they are at doing any of these, but that's another story).

For the first time, in addition to your work product, you are now responsible for the work of others. When many people are handed this opportunity, the inclination is to be very prescriptive in moving the work forward.

Then one morning you wake up and realize that there may be a different way to make it happen.

How so? Due to being given more responsibilities or seeing that the team indeed has the capabilities to get their work done without you looking over their shoulders, you realize that you don't have to actively manage every element of the process. In this sense, you actually take a step forward in your leadership journey by taking a step back.

Sometimes this step is taken consciously. Other times not. When done consciously, often there is some discomfort.

The Highs and Lows of Being Tapped to Lead

When one is asked to manage a process or a team, it is usually a straightforward request. However, we often get thrown into our early leadership roles without really realizing what is happening. From the emotional high of, *"Wow, they recognize that I can add value beyond my task."* to the sheer terror of, *"What are these folks who are on my team all responsible for? Can they do it with the resources they have? How am I, the rookie, supposed to keep the train on the tracks and moving forward at an acceptable pace?"*

As a manager, most of the time, we know specifically what our team is responsible for. We usually know who to get inputs from and where our output is supposed to go. However, as the responsibilities increase and become broader, the expectations become more nebulous and the list is not as complete.

As I have coached new leaders, one of the questions I am often asked is: *"How do you actually get to a true list of both deliverables and expectations?"*

In larger organizations, there is usually a fairly detailed job description. However, this too is often not the complete list. Frankly, while the job description is a great starting point, it does not fully answer the question because as leaders, we have moved to positions where we are both leading and, as members of larger teams, we are *following* as well. While we can look to our boss to obtain his or her expectations, we also have to look to our peers and members of the teams that we are leading to obtain their expectations too.

What Are You Responsible For?

So how do you find "The List" of responsibilities? To quote Ghostbusters, *"Who you gonna call?"* As stated, you need to reach out to lots of folks.

Inevitably, some of the data gathered will be contradictory. So it is critical to understand that another one of the skills that is being developed at this point relates to **filtering.** That is, what data do you accept from which source?

Another important piece of developing understanding is, one hopes, that most folks will not intentionally mislead you. Rather, they are providing you with their perspectives on the questions that you have asked. They are giving you the information that they believe you have requested that they have already filtered, consciously or unconsciously.

A crucial insight here is that just because someone's information is not correct the first time doesn't mean that they are intentionally *trying* to mislead. That said, let's say that you find on the second, third and fourth time you ask for information from the individual that you are still getting bad data. In that event, it might be time to consider whether they understand the questions you are asking and the expectations that you have for them regarding them doing their jobs.

As you have determined what your team is supposed to do, it should become more obvious about where you are dependent on other parts of the organization and where they are dependent on you.

Tracking Information

Now, it's time to develop another roadmap. One hopes that when you start in a new job, unless it is a brand new or newly reorganized organization, the information flows have been identified. However, for a number of reasons, not the least of which are the personalities of the people involved, the old information flows, both incoming and outgoing, may have changed.

It is critical, both early and often, to take the time to look at this to ensure that all involved with the information still understand and agree with the flows as you have captured them.

So, we have conquered Step One and now know the responsibilities of our team. We know what information we get from whom and what information we are responsible for providing to others and when they expect to receive it.

Taking a step back, though, how much different is this from managing a process?

"Understand that all people have different motivations. Natural leaders get people excited about ideas and get people to want to do them."

Kevin Mott, Financial Advisor, Edward Jones

Who Is On The Team?

The progression into leadership happens as we start to understand how to deal with the individuals on our teams.

In the initial chapter, we mentioned the notion of Adaptive Leadership. While we each have our own dominant leadership styles, one type does truly not fit all members of any team.

It is not uncommon to have:

➢ **Some team members who want to be told how, when and where to do each activity.**

➢ **Other team members who want to see that their work is being approved while not being directly watched.**

➢ **Still other team members who want to be given an objective and the flexibility to accomplish it.**

As an Insightful and Adaptive Leader, it is necessary to take the time to truly understand what each member of the team needs in the form of leadership and at least have an appreciation for what each individual wants.

As with any exercise that includes people and personalities, there are inevitably landmines that will be encountered in the journey. These can include things as simple as being a graduate of the "wrong" school. It can be as complex as having been brought into the position and leapfrogging someone who had thought that the job was theirs.

It is incumbent on Insightful Leaders to recognize that these landmines exist and determine if and how they should be addressed, all while keeping the organization's responsibilities well in sight.

Staci Scharadin
CEO
Diamond Wealth Management

Staci didn't "get started" as a leader because the reality is that leadership has always been in her DNA. From owning a carpet cleaning company to opening a catering business, Staci worked three jobs for most of her life – that is, until 1994, when she was recruited into the financial services industry. Staci became the CEO of Diamond Wealth Management after evolving and ultimately purchasing an independent firm named WallStreet Financial Services. She views Diamond as a wealth management firm where planning rather than transactions drive results.

As you move from a management position to a leadership role, I think you constantly need to take a look at yourself to evaluate your approach. For example, if we have a role within our firm that has had a great deal of turnover, I'll examine the pattern of how I hire. I'll also ask if I'm inspiring people versus telling them what to do. Am I providing the "why" behind the "what?" Am I micromanaging to a fault? Are my standards too high or is it what my clients deserve? Of course, it's the latter. But these are important questions you must ask yourself as a CEO when it takes so much to earn the trust of a client who is wealthy and successful. If someone on your team drops the ball, you have to hold yourself accountable too.

When you open your own business, you set a vision for the firm, hire employees, implement processes and more. You become a CEO. But in all honesty, I didn't sign up to be CEO. I don't mind setting a direction, but I am more prone to put my ego down than want to go through a lot of daily minutiae related to HR. In the process, I've found that I can actually be an industry leader without being an organizational leader. You don't have to be in love with all aspects of being a CEO, other than certain critical pieces associated with vision, for example.

Finally, as you become a leader, don't let perfect be the enemy of good. Now, this doesn't mean you have to tolerate an "OK" job but perfection is not essential. Also, remember to stick to what you're best at so you can keep your organization tight and focused. There will be a constant pull to expand your offerings and add roles. As tempting as it can be to say "yes" to many things, you need to learn to continually say "no" so you can keep those things that distract you out of the picture.

TAKEAWAYS

❖ Learning how to manage is a step in learning how to lead, but not the only step.

❖ Moving from managing an organization to leading an organization will not happen without work and perhaps some discomfort.

❖ Each job is often much more than what is spelled out in the job description.

❖ It is necessary to both understand how you are comfortable leading and how your team members want and need to be led.

EXERCISES

For most of us, before we are given the opportunity to lead an organization, we are given the opportunity to take on the role of managing a group. Understanding the different expectations of management versus leadership can be key in one's career progression.

In our first exercise:

❖ Describe the responsibilities of being manager of a team charged with preparing one element or sub element of your organization's product.

❖ Describe who your likely peers are and to whom you report.

❖ Describe what changes when you are given responsibility for preparing more than one element of the product or the entire organizational product.

❖ Describe the roles of your likely peers, your boss and your key subordinates.

❖ Describe how the increased responsibilities change your role from managing to leading.

In our second exercise, as an example, you have just been named the leader of a team whose responsibility it is to prepare a market entry plan for a new product that your company is offering. The plan needs to be completed for presentation to the Board 90 days after you start the job.

However, consider each of the following scenarios for how you have gotten this position.

❖ In one, you have been promoted from within the group.
❖ In another, you have been promoted from another group.
❖ In the third, you have been hired into this role from outside the company.

Now, consider a situation where you have been given a new role with an output required at a specific point in time.

❖ Describe your 14, 30 and 60-day objectives in the role.

❖ Describe who you will seek input from in accomplishing your objectives.

DECISION MATRIX QUESTIONS

❖ Do I understand what we are responsible for? Does the team?

❖ Do I understand how we fit in the organization? Does the team?

❖ Do I understand the individuals on my team?

❖ Do I understand the intra- and inter-team dynamics?

Becoming and Being a Learning Leader

"I wish that someone had told me mistakes are OK to make – as long as you learn from them, fix your approach and move on."

Mike Folz, Principal, Balasa Dinverno Foltz

When you assume a leadership role, rarely, if ever, are you given a complete set of directions of how to make the team work through teamwork.

While you may be handed a fairly comprehensive map of how the team fits within the overall organization, you won't always be given a clear picture of the strengths and weaknesses of the members of your team. Even if you are handed an excellent assessment, there's usually at least one element in doubt – namely, how is the team going to **survive** and **thrive** with you at the helm?

Let's take a quick look at these two notions. To **survive** is defined as to *continue to live or exist, especially in spite of danger or hardship.* To **thrive** is defined as *to prosper or flourish.*

With these definitions in mind, how do you as the leader act when leading the team in a thriving atmosphere? How does that differ for you when it's a survival atmosphere?

In addition, we have to consider the personal situations and dynamics of the individuals on the team. Not only must we constantly pay attention to our team members and what they need, but we also need to be able to modify our personal styles to fit the realities of the situations that we are facing. This relates to being an Insightful Leader.

"Roller Coaster" Leadership: From Survive To Thrive

In the first international deal that I led after I joined Motorola, I got to experience the highs and lows of roller coaster leadership firsthand.

I was leading a small team that included some direct reports as well as some folks on temporary assignment from other groups. We were tasked with creating a joint venture with a subsidiary of Telefonica to manufacture cellular network equipment in and for Spain. When successful, this was going to allow Motorola to displace Ericsson as the main equipment provider for Telefonica's next generation cellular network.

Over the course of seven months of negotiations, I was told on *three separate occasions* by my counterpart that the deal was off. Talk about being in survival mode.

The first time I was told that the deal was off, I immediately called my boss and gave him the news. I also quickly told my team and thanked them for their hard work, had a great dinner in Madrid and then headed back to Chicago the next morning. When I got to the office, my boss said, "*Hold on.*" While I was in transit, some of the deal parameters had changed and the deal was back on. Now I had to reconvene the team and get everyone revved back up.

The second and third time we were told that the deal was off, I told the team, but also suggested that folks not plan to get into any new projects. I hoped that any changed parameters would be from the other side, but I also hoped that we would find a way to make the deal happen. In both cases, we got rolling again in a couple of weeks and were able to finalize the deal.

As we moved from "survive" to "thrive," we could see the very real possibility that we would displace one of our major competitors, assuring the company of generating millions of dollars of sales over the next several years.

Live and Learn and Lead

I learned from this experience that, even when I was down, my boss had my back and would look for ways to make the right things happen. I also learned how to keep my team engaged, even when we had seemingly hit a wall.

Reflecting on it, I can understand how this shaped my approach in dealing with teams as we rolled through the ups and downs of business. In this case, we were fortunate that no one on the team had any personal crisis to deal with as we were riding the roller coaster. Still, I was becoming attuned to the nuances of my team and could see that there were some storms brewing that ended up having to be taken care of at a later date. I was also fortunate as I was able to focus all of my attention on this single deal.

We all have been in situations over time where some things are going superbly and others, well, not so much. You may have to deal with team members who have sick family members as well as other family crises, for example. In every case, if you're the leader of the team, **the key to getting through the situation is to listen and understand what the team members need.** Then you can create a road map for accommodating those needs within the context of the team's overall goals.

"My father was my mentor, but he practiced MBY or Manage By Yelling. There was a great deal of collateral damage. Then he realized the fundamental question, which is: Would you want to be treated that way?"

Jim Flanagan, CEO and Owner, Nuance Solutions

Listening

Through the course of writing this book, I have asked countless senior leaders from all types of corporate and non-profit enterprises:

"When you were starting out as a leader, what is the one piece of advice that you wish you had been given or were given but just did not understand at the time?"

While there were many answers, the most common theme I heard was that these leaders were told early on to **listen to those around them.** This included not only the people they worked for and with, but also those who worked for them.

Furthermore, they talked about the need to both ask questions and to listen to and understand the questions that are being asked of them.

Today, I make no excuses for my curiosity. While I have never been shy about asking folks "how" and "why," one piece of bad advice that I got at one point was that I should not wear this curious nature so blatantly on my sleeve.

However, as Tom Wilson, CEO of Allstate points out, *"When one goes to higher levels in an organization, your question-to-statement ratio should also go up."*

When it's OK to Say: *"I Don't Know."*

Another piece of the puzzle for me has been the willingness to admit when I do not know the answer to a question. **Being able to say to your peers, your boss and the folks who work for you that you don't know the answer to a question is an important part of one's leadership growth journey.**

However, when saying I don't know, it is critical to be able to then say, *"I will find out."*

Saying *"I don't know"* to a question that deals with the status of your team's deliverables and performance is <u>not</u> what is being discussed here (if you don't know the answers to those questions, you are probably in the wrong place). Rather, these questions are broader and deal with areas that are probably outside the normal purview of you and your team.

To grow as a Learning and Insightful Leader, one needs to be comfortable delving into new and different areas typically that are outside the normal scope of operations.

Seeking Feedback

In order to continue to improve one's leadership skills and abilities, one needs to continue to understand their own personal strengths and weaknesses. While getting a review from your supervisor is great, the impact of **unvarnished feedback from your peers and those who work for you can be a personal force multiplier.** The key is once you have the feedback...what do you do with it?

One of the commonly discussed theories in sports today is that you focus your development efforts on improving the areas where you are strong. While this may very well be the case, in order to play in the pros, all areas of your game need to be at a very high level and you need to have those one or two places where you can really shine as well. This may deal with analytical capabilities, but it is also relevant for the soft skills of leadership as well.

Ralph Waldo Emerson isn't often credited with writing about leadership, but this quote from him does sum it up:

"The speed of the leader determines the rate of the pack."

Pedro A. Guerrero
CEO
Guerrero

For the last dozen years, Pedro has led Guerrero, a 90-person independent media company focused on recognizing and promoting executives in eight industry-focused brands. The company's content caters to a range of senior-level audiences from attorneys to builders to Hispanic executives.

Ours is very much a millennial company in that the average age is about 26 years old. Even the middle management is young and relatively inexperienced in management. The positive side of that is that you're talking about people who want to be part of something bigger than themselves. They're motivated, eager and smart individuals who have a thirst for learning. That's a challenge for us in leadership because unfortunately, we've found the speed of the learning curve isn't always the fastest. So how do we scale up our leadership experience to impact our middle management layer?

Luckily, we're a culture that reads. The organizational management books that my leadership team and I read are at the front desk so that everyone who comes in will read the same one or two books that we use to run the business. We expect everyone who begins with our company, even those in junior positions, to read the same books that the leadership team is reading. That way, they understand the same language we're using.

In addition, I think learning through better and more frequent communication is important. So beyond the weekly and quarterly meetings, we have a monthly "Town Hall," a company-wide meeting where we update the staff with headlines and status updates on important company projects. Even with all that we've implemented, there's a lot of information that can remain unknown. So I want to do everything in our power to broadcast achievements and updates to the entire company on a regular basis as well as naturally get input from our people too.

TAKEAWAYS

❖ The team works best when there is a high level of teamwork.

❖ We need to lead both in the "thrive" as well as the "survive" mode and be able to adapt our leadership styles accordingly.

❖ Even when things at work seem fine, as a leader you have to be tuned in to other elements of your team's lives in order to lead them effectively.

❖ Saying "*I don't know*" can be a strength in the right environment. It is even better when followed with, "*But I will find out.*"

❖ Seek feedback and then make and execute the plan to do something with what you have heard.

EXERCISES

❖ Think of one area of your business where you are having a challenge.

Some examples of these issues might be:

  ➤ An unexpected and persistent fall off in sales.
  ➤ A long-time customer suddenly and without warning closes its doors.
  ➤ Your expenses going up in three areas unexpectedly and suddenly.

❖ Now, with the issue that you have identified, list 5 possible courses of action.

❖ For each action identified, be sure to include resources, people, and money required to implement the action. Then identify ranking criteria for the identified actions and rank them.

❖ Also, in each case, classify a group of people who will help you to identify, quantify and rank the actions.

❖ Before assembling the team, identify and prioritize the skills and experiences you want as part of the team. Then identify which of those you absolutely need in order to get the ball moving and address the open questions. At this point, you can start assembling the team.

❖ So, with these steps done, *what are you waiting for to get moving?*

DECISION MATRIX QUESTIONS

❖ What types of questions am I not comfortable asking?

❖ What types of questions am I not comfortable being asked?

❖ Are there people/functional disciplines in my organization I need to learn how to communicate with?

5

Peaks, Valleys and Plateaus of Leadership

"You have to work to get people to put the bags of bricks down."

Jim Ford, National Director of Market Development
Trendway Corporation

I'd like you to think back to the very first time that you were given the responsibility for leading a team. Remember what that felt like? Chances are, you can probably recall the good parts rather easily.

Now think a little deeper about the *other* aspects of becoming a leader that you weren't so excited about. The increased responsibility. The prospect of moving into uncharted territory for your career. You undoubtedly felt a fair amount of fear and trepidation as so many leaders often do (but don't like to admit).

As the leadership experience evolves, you'll remember the first time your team was recognized for excellent service, the first time that your team wasn't recognized and the first time that your team did not live up to any expectation.

This ebb-and-flow of wins and losses is common for us to embed into our memory banks, but we all too often care to recall the peaks first and foremost. Why? Yes, it makes us feel better to think of the positive experiences, but it has been evident over the years that **there is just as much to learn from the valleys and plateaus as there is from hitting the peaks.**

If we can understand how we internalize these negative experiences as well as how we work with our teams to get them to learn from such steps backward, it might be as rewarding a lesson as what our successes taught us – perhaps even more so.

It's why an important piece of being an Insightful Leader comes from understanding that the journey forward will include peaks, valleys and plateaus. Goals will be reached while other times we will stall and not be able to make it up to that targeted peak. We can learn so much from both experiences.

I took the attitude a long time ago that if I wanted to be a better, more insightful leader, I would learn from everyone I worked for. Even if that someone was a less than an optimal boss because it is as important to learn what NOT to do as it is to learn what to do.

"Leaders authorize the style of the organization."

Lawrence Aaron, CEO, Great American Finance

What Did We Learn From That?

Let's imagine that you're facing the daunting challenge of climbing a mountain. Before you lie two paths: On one hand, you can go up the steepest path to get up to the top quickly or on the other hand, you can take the more roundabout path that isn't as steep and will take longer.

Does it sound like a no-brainer to choose the steep path? Maybe. Yet if you choose the roundabout option, you may be able to learn things that you wouldn't otherwise learn. You don't have to worry as much about slipping off the path and dying by going this path. Now you can go around and say, *"In the course of going up this hill, I can take my time. I can take in more animals and views of nature that I'd never have seen before."* Suddenly, your path is more satisfying because it's not just about climbing the mountain.

The Valleys Can Teach Us Plenty Too

Before I got to Motorola, I worked at an independent telephone company that was just getting into the cable television industry. After six years, I moved into a business unit involved with leasing phone equipment – a switch I didn't exactly see coming but I remained flexible and enjoyed this new group I was in. In time, I was sure that we would see that business unit grow and it was clear we were building a significant portfolio. Everything was going terrifically.

That is, until THE phone call came.

Our senior leaders of the business unit were sitting in a staff meeting and got a phone call that the company wanted to get out of the particular leasing business our unit dealt with.

Suddenly, our reason for being...didn't exist anymore.

There we were, sitting around a conference room table, thinking about what had just happened. Not long after that moment, I had to think about how I wanted to redefine myself. I had been offered a role where I had to consider going a level down from where I was. I could take that job.

Or maybe...just maybe...I could do something about it by finding another job.

In looking for another job, I saw an ad in the Wall Street Journal for a position at Motorola. I applied for the job, possessing two out of three requirements they were looking for (couldn't hurt to try, right?). Soon after I sent in my application and resume, I realized that I had some friends from The Kellogg School of Management at Northwestern University at Motorola too. One of those friends said, *"Let me see what I can find out about the job."*

This would lead to an interview that would lead to me being offered the job and what would be the beginning of a wonderful 17-year portion of my career.

Think of it. There you are, at the depths of despair, discovering your job no longer exists and the only way you can stay on in the company is to take a *demotion*. Right after that, you're given a golden opportunity at a growing company with the chance to travel internationally on a regular basis.

The funny part of the story – my friend who put in a good word for me and encouraged me to pursue the job? Many years later, I would learn that *he applied for the job too!* I had no idea. This brings us to one of the key marks of an Insightful Leader: **At times, you're going to do things that aren't in your self-interest in the short-term. You're going to do it because it's just the right thing to do for the environment you're in.**

Learning from losing is not in any way meant to say that we should strive for less than a successful outcome. Rather, it means that we need to keep our eyes and ears open to learning from those less desirable outcomes.

There's a famous saying of, *"Winning isn't everything. It's the only thing."* That may be so, but do you also know *why* you lost? So you didn't get the engagement. Do you have the guts to look at why you lost the deal? Was the loss because someone bid lower than you or was it due to an element of your presentation? Was it because your product was inferior? Are you in the right market for your product?

Wins Are Not the Endgame.
They're Stages of the Journey.

It can feel good to celebrate the wins. Go ahead and do so. However, I encourage you to "reserve" some of that energy for when the time comes that you have just lost.

I'll give you an example: I was passing by a group from another business unit that was celebrating like there was no tomorrow. They'd worked hard to win some new business and weren't holding back.

That's when I called over the leader of the group. *"Congratulations, it's a marvelous win. But you know, you might want to bottle some of this enthusiasm in your team,"* I said. He, of course, looked at me like I was crazy. Yet, intrigued, he asked why I'd want his team to take it easy now. *"Well, because there are going to be times when you lose and when you do, you'll be glad that you've reserved some of this energy for that day to tide you over."* He quickly dismissed this notion with a wave of his hand. That was another problem for another day.

Sure enough, that day I'd predicted, the one of a big loss, came soon enough. It wasn't that I took any pleasure in seeing that team down, of course. Still, it wasn't easy for that business unit to get over. After so much energy expended on the giant win, it was hard for them to summon anything to pick themselves back up after a setback.

The Insightful Leader must always remember that **wins are part of the journey and the journey is *iterative*.** If your goal is to win the World Series after 108 years of losing like the Chicago Cubs, that's great. However, is the goal really to win it just once? Or is it to establish a culture where we're going to understand what it takes to win continuously?

There is a bigger picture of wins and losses in that both are teachers for leaders and their teams. Only by applying the lessons from our peaks **and valleys** will we be able to advance through the plateaus and achieve great things together as a team.

Helen Levinson
CEO and Founder
Indigo Interactive, Inc.

For the last 20 years, Helen has been seeking innovative ways to deploy technology to streamline business processes. Today, as head of Indigo Interactive, she leads a team of creative and passionate technologists who build quality assurance and compliance software for accrediting organizations. One of her firm's newest products, Jura Accreditation Management System, takes the time, expense and paper out of organizational workflows.

Sometimes I don't really see myself as a leader but rather someone who is very stubborn and tenacious, pushing forward to get what I want. Even with that quality, I went through a significant "valley" in my career when I separated from my business partner. That separation would ultimately be a year-long fight and wasn't without a degree of damage to my reputation. When I finally emerged from that experience by starting Indigo, you'd think I'd have turned a page but there was plenty of issues to overcome there too.

For one, I wasn't doing enough listening at Indigo to my key people. I was operating the business in knee-jerk reaction way trying to solve problems rather than being proactive about it.

Then came the real compelling moment in which I knew I had to press the "reset button" in my professional life. As I was noticing a number of female engineers were leaving the company and being replaced by male engineers, I discovered that my CIO at the time was gossiping about me to the team, which created a completely toxic environment.

If that wasn't bad enough, even as we were growing and adding new staff members, some of the older staff members were trying to "poison the well" with toxic behavior around those new staff members as well. Something had to give and quickly. So I put a plan in place to change over the staff. Of 17 of us, we pushed out 13 staff members over the course of a year. Suddenly, we were sitting there with a ton of projects in front of us and not a lot of resources to handle them. So we had to pull together to figure out what our most critical problems were and solve them one by one.

As soon as we pushed out the last "bad apples" of the bunch, everybody was much happier, collaborating more often and more motivated to succeed. For the most part, our reputation is as high as it's ever been and we're now one of the leading software vendors in the U.S. in this market. The best revenge to anyone who has been the boulder in my life is success.

If you can remain steady amongst the turmoil around you, you have an excellent chance of pulling through the "valley" period that many leaders experience and rarely avoid.

TAKEAWAYS

❖ Celebrate your wins, but remember to "reserve" some of that celebratory energy for when times are not so good.

❖ Most of us don't wander through the "Valleys" of loss forever. Losing is natural. Accept it in order to shore up the team for your next advance.

❖ The key question after a loss is to ask, "What did we learn from that experience, what could we have done differently and what will we do differently next time?"

❖ Don't just do a post-mortem meeting. Moving forward means that you have applied the lessons from both winning and losing. And that doesn't often keep you in a plateau for long.

EXERCISES

❖ Identify a "valley" situation where you did not meet the objectives.

❖ Develop 3 bullet points that will be used in a team meeting to talk about why the objective was missed

❖ Develop 3 bullet points to talk about the way forward.

❖ Identify a "plateau" situation.

❖ Develop 3 bullet points that will be used in a team meeting to talk about the plateau.

❖ Develop 3 bullet points to talk about the way forward.

DECISION MATRIX QUESTIONS

❖ What are the takeaways from coming in second or last?

❖ Do we believe we can dust ourselves off easily and get on with life? Why or why not? What do we need to change to avoid this again?

❖ What are the takeaways from coming in first?

❖ Do those who come in first express humility at the same time?

6

Leadership at the Speed of Life

"Work is the means to building a real life.
Earn so that you can do."

Michael Rosengarden, President, Autohaus Automotive

The concept of seeking "work-life balance" is meant to address that there is a proper way to prioritize between what you do at work to advance your career compared to the time that you are devoting to important aspects of your personal life – activities related to your family, general leisure, health and spiritual development.

What impacts and potentially threatens this balance? Two things.

> ➢ *One, as an emerging leader **advances in an organization** and takes on more leadership*

responsibilities, there are more demands placed on the individual for their participation, advice and counsel. I've witnessed that firsthand and seen it happen to colleagues.

> *Secondly, most of us are always on and "**omni-connected**" through our mobile communications devices, whether we are at the top or bottom of an organization. We're usually expected to be always available and thinking about the current issues at work. When something, anything pops up in our inbox or on our voicemail, we have to be ready to address it.*

From Balance to "Work-Life Blend"

The second factor I mentioned, the connectivity element, plays a big role in why many of my conversations have moved from a work-life balance toward a **work-life blend**.

In a world where our phones – and by association, our email – are rarely, if ever, turned off, there is less separation of work and the rest of our lives than ever. If we want to, we can check our work email as soon as we wake up, on the train, walking to the office, etc. Even when we are at meetings outside of work, we almost can't help but attempt to check on work-related issues.

Being a Baby Boomer myself, I often think about how our particular generation engages in this "always on" mentality when, for most of our lives, we did not have such instant, almost universal access.

However, other generations certainly have this behavior. In fact, as I interviewed a variety of leaders for this book, many of whom are Generation Xers or Millennials, they agree that this is an issue.

Yet they also believe that they are starting to wrest back control of their lives.

Is It A Friday Afternoon Or Monday Morning Issue?

In one of my early positions, our company was working on a transaction to buy a cable television franchise from its owners in Florida. We were making progress on the deal when, mid-day on a Friday, we received a request for some additional analysis and information from one of the senior people in the corporation.

I frantically sought out my boss to tell him about the request and to get his advice on how – not when – to respond.

His first words to me were, *"Is this a Friday afternoon problem or a Monday morning one?"*

I had no idea what he meant.

> *A Friday afternoon problem, he explained, is one that needs to immediately be addressed. It's a problem that can't wait. The kind that we should work whatever hours are necessary to get the answer as soon as humanly possible.*

> *A Monday morning problem, on the other hand, is one that we can do some work on the afternoon it arises, but we can also leave it until Monday to fully dig into it.*

This insight, for me, began to lay the foundation for how to balance work and life.

To this day, when I am confronted with significant issues, independent of the day of the week or time of day when the issue is presented, I stop to think about whether it is a Friday afternoon or a Monday morning issue. This extends to issues at work, at home and in my work in the community.

Consequently, to be effective as a leader, you need to have your own priorities in order while being able to relate to the priorities of your team members.

What's Important to You?
Have you thought about how you answer that question?

> ➤ Is it your work?
> ➤ Your family?
> ➤ Your friends?
> ➤ The role you play in your community?
> ➤ Is it some element of alone time?

The answer for most of us to all of these questions is: **Yes.**

It's not necessarily easy to balance your own priorities. Understanding how these factors play into decisions being made by members of your team is even more difficult and is a critical leadership skill.

As both individuals and as leaders, how do we balance the demands that our family, community and workplace have on us? At the same time, how do we set the expectations for our teams? These issues face us throughout the lifecycle of our organization as well as the lifecycle of our career.

Unfortunately, there will be times when one or more of the legs (family, community, work, friends, self) may have to take a back seat. We as leaders need to make sure that our organization understands that, while we have an appreciation of individual circumstances, at times work has to come first.

How to Set and Communicate Priorities

When making decisions regarding these priorities for ourselves, what is the message we want to send and actually do send to the organization when there is too much weight placed on one of these factors?

Robert Hughes, a retired US Army Colonel and now a member of the faculty of the Kellogg School of Management's Executive Education program, offered the following during an interview for this book:

> *"Optics matter. That is, that you need to walk the talk. As a leader in an office setting that is not supposed to be always on, you should not expect that anyone would be there before you in the morning or after you at night. In fact, you need to make it clear what the expectations are and 'help' people adhere to them."*

Start By Taking Back Time from the Devices in Your Life

It used to be that when you sent a letter or made a call, you wouldn't know if you would get a response. Now, we have come to expect that when a call is made, it will be answered or returned very quickly. The same is true for emails and text messages.

While quick response is key, Insightful Leaders feel the need to turn off devices occasionally so they can focus on what is important as opposed to what is *apparently* urgent. Doing this and giving the team the right to do this as well is key to leading effective teams.

When "All Hands On Deck" Is Appropriate (And When It Isn't)

Insightful Leaders make every attempt to address individual circumstances but when push comes to shove, they also know how to communicate to the team that more than just attention is needed. When the situation warrants it, the team's attention AND presence are required. The key for leaders is understanding what triggers out-of-the-ordinary events so they can work with the entire team.

> *"With multiple generations currently in the workforce, you need to constantly learn and re-learn how to attack what people want and their expectations."*

Pat McKune, CFO, M. Holland Company

The Culture Statement

Groups of people, whether in formal or informal organizations, develop a culture in which they operate. For many companies, a great deal of time is spent thinking about and **writing down a statement regarding the culture and the expectations of the individuals who will be part of it.**

The operative word in that last sentence is "expectations." It's such a key foundation of the culture statement because when a company articulates a statement about what it expects the culture to be and has been clear about the work/life blend of those who work for the company, a lot of ambiguity should be diminished.

This can be wonderful when people buy into it and a rapid decline of the organization when people don't. While it is not a guarantee of a more positive outcome, the leader needs to buy in and walk the talk – because if that doesn't happen, from anyone at the senior level – the company is often on a collision course with big issues.

What Planet Are You From?

As your leadership journey continues and the members of your teams change, getting a greater perspective into work-life blend can be one of your biggest challenges.

I have been fortunate to spend time working in many countries around the world and have had the opportunity to get to know people from these countries well. These friends quickly helped me understand that their views of work/life blend and balance varied significantly from ours.

As my responsibilities evolved, I was fortunate to have these people to talk through issues with. The understanding of the importance of a company culture was key. We then laid this concept over the culture of the country we were in, making sure that all knew what was acceptable and what wasn't.

A WORD FROM AN INSIGHTFUL LEADER

Joe Flanagan
Chairman and CEO
Acquirent

For over 25 years, Joe's ability to sell has transformed a variety of businesses, including his own. After striking out on his own at just 27 years old, he built JP Flanagan Corporation into one of Chicago's largest insurance agencies. He then sold that business and founded Acquirent, an outsourced sales and marketing company that has been hired by such businesses as Humana and Enterprise Rent-A-Car that are passionate about augmenting their sales capabilities for stronger results. Today, Joe has grown Acquirent to a 110-person firm that has been named to the Inc. 5000 several times.

I've been fortunate in my life to be able to drive an incredible business, have a phenomenal family and stay very involved in my community. If there's any secret I've found to keeping all of that in balance while still going to work with a smile on my face, it's having the guidance of people closest to me whose opinions I trust.

In my career, I've had the ability to assemble a group of outside professionals such as lawyers, accountants, dealmakers and other people I call upon regularly to be my individual Board of Directors. They are invaluable resources whenever I'm facing a big challenge.

When you get to crucial decision points as a leader, it's important that you pull together the people in your life who deeply understand who you are and what you value in terms of your work, your family, your social life, your needs for work-life balance and more. You need to make a presentation to that group about these factors. Let them ask you questions and guide you to clarity. That's what I've done in my life. When it comes to those people, I trust their judgment because all they care about is what's best for me and my family. There's no financial incentive in it for them. They love me and genuinely want to see me successful. So I'm grateful for being able to attract people whose opinions I trust to help guide me.

As you build this kind of support structure yourself, I don't recommend that you bring together people just to talk – always make sure you're coming together for a *defined purpose*. At the same time, once you define that purpose, you don't necessarily need to handle all aspects of the meeting on your own. These are your real allies we're talking about, so feel free to lean on one of them to do things for you like run the meeting, for example. Having been on the other side of the table as a member of someone else's individual Board of Directors, I've had the pleasure of serving as a moderator to elicit questions from the group and gather comments. In the process of doing so, there's an immense satisfaction in doing your part to help "lift the clouds" for someone you care about.

TAKEAWAYS

❖ Is it a Friday afternoon or Monday morning issue? We need to be able to understand and communicate to our team when an issue or question needs to be dealt with NOW or can wait until tomorrow.

❖ Seek to understand what is important, make sure others do and then understand and communicate that sometimes the priorities need to change.

❖ Take control back from "Always On" and make sure that your team understands what they can do, with the caveat that emergencies happen and priorities might change.

❖ Seek to define and live culture. Communicate that culture can and will change. Communicate and encourage evolution and enrichment of the culture statement and encourage your team to tell you when your actions are not living up to the words.

EXERCISES

❖ List the five most important elements of where you want to spend your time (for example: Work, community service, introspection, friends, family).

❖ Rank these elements in order of importance to you. Then list the percentage of time spent on each.

❖ With each, identify factors that may lead to a temporary change in priority.

Now answer the following:

> ➤ Does your team understand what is important to you?
> ➤ Does your family?
> ➤ Can your team honestly go through the same exercise and share it with their peers? With their Supervisors? With their teams?

As this exercise gets more fully embedded throughout the organization, everyone should become more comfortable with living through the issues that come with leading and being led at the speed of life.

DECISION MATRIX QUESTIONS

❖ Do I want to be part of or lead an organization that requires the rest of the team, as well as me, to always be on?

❖ Do I walk the talk and require my team to live the way I want to regarding work/life blend?

❖ Do I understand the generational differences, apparent and inherent, in the teams that I am leading?

7

The Journey Continues From Leading to Advising

"As an effective Board Member, you need to learn the 'nose in, fingers out' style. That is, you can be interested in what is going on, but it is not up to you to meddle and fix it."

Dennis Kessler, President, Midwest Business Advisors

In previous chapters, we've talked about the importance of work-life balance, which we now refer to as *"work-life blend."* Leaders who understand how to bring together their own blend of family, workplace, community and so forth stand to have a profound impact on how they lead a company.

How so? If the leader can *"fix their own house"* in this way, he or she will have great empathy for employees who face their own unique set of work-life blend obstacles and in turn, will become that much better of a leader of others. Because those people will invite the leader to come help fix *their* house!

That's when a funny thing happens: **Suddenly, you're more than a leader. You're an *advisor*.** You know that in leadership mode, you've been expected to lead the execution of plans in order to accomplish goals. But what does it mean to be asked to give advice to a team as opposed to being a leader? How does that change the dynamic, if at all, between you and your team?

Yes, there is a personal fulfillment from being asked for counsel. At the same time, one needs to understand how being exposed to issues from a different perspective can increase your impact as an Insightful Leader.

Not every leader can make the journey from leading to advising with ease. When approached for advice, the very question can throw certain leaders off guard. It may cause you to ask yourself, *"Am I being asked for advice...":*

➢ Because of my title and the expectation that I have something to offer?

➢ Because the person asking has been told that they need to ask me and doesn't know or understand that I may actually have something to offer?

➢ Because the person doing the asking understands the value that I bring to the situation at hand?

First, it's important to understand that there are different ways to contribute advice. Mentoring others on your team is one example of this opportunity. Another opportunity to give advice can come when you are asked to sit on a Board in which you might install a leader of a company and help set the long-term objectives for the business.

When you're doing things like that, you're creating larger boundaries for you to operate within. Beyond leading, you can now have the responsibility for mentoring and being a resource when someone runs into a brick wall of a challenge.

"You have to be able to call on experience without being condescending."

Bruce Breitzman, President, Spartan Light Metal Products

It's a subtle but crucial difference in this delivery, in which you're openly saying, *"I have experience in this area and I can provide some insights"* or *"Tell me about what's going on..."* or *"Have you thought about..."*

It's not *"I have experience in this area and this is how I would do it."*

See the difference?

In the first example, with more open questions and statements, the leader is setting the table for a reasonable two-way interaction to occur that consists of offering some options for the employee's or fellow Board member's consideration. The leader isn't pushing anyone this way or that.

The latter example is much less so – it's a leader who is instructing how to go about making changes according to their own personal approach and experience.

What can an Insightful Leader do to set the expectation that asking for advice is welcome and that they have something to offer?

So often, we hear a leader say, *"Well, my door is always open! Come to me for anything!"*

We can do better than giving people that kind of "status update" and then going about our business. Let me give you an example.

I recently became the Treasurer of a non-profit in my community in part due to the former Treasurer knowing my capabilities. He said, *"I trust Dave because I see how he operates, even when he doesn't have the specific answer."*

Do I have all the experience associated with a role like this? No. But I have a comfort with the issues to the point where people say, *"We know he's not going to let us get too far astray. He'll push the pause button when we need him to."*

Mind you, I'm just a Board member. There's still a Director of Finance of the organization who's actually doing all the work! But I **set the expectation that I was here to be a resource** for him. He knows that I am the one who can be there when he asks, *"What do you think about that?"* He also understands that as an advisor, I'm helping him chart a course but I'm still not responsible for the actual doing of tasks like he is.

So the Insightful Leader must do more than take the *"I'm here if you need me"* approach if people are going to feel comfortable entrusting them as a partner to find clarity and a way forward on a problem.

Does that comfort level happen overnight? No. Don't be surprised if it takes time and patience.

Let's say a recent hire at a company has questions about the way certain decisions in their department have been made. They're about to approach their manager, simply to get more information.

That's when a long-time employee stops them in the hallway and tells them not to even think about it. Why? Because it's just never been that way "around here." Employees do what they're told here and keep their heads down without questioning the management. Never mind that this person's manager may have actually *welcomed* the conversation and seen their employee in a new and positive light.

When you have that kind of history and precedent to overcome, changing the culture isn't impossible but certainly can be a challenge. If you've ever attempted to move an initiative fast through some larger corporations, you know how that can go. You're likely to get questions like, *"Why do you want to do that? We've never done it that way before."*

Nonetheless, the Insightful Leader isn't deterred by history.

If you extend yourself to your team and work at it regularly to consistently communicate with them, you will gradually reinforce the notion that you are a person that they can go to in order to discuss certain issues. A few years ago, this was called "Managing by Walking Around." If you say it and then you do it, the foundation is there. Keep at it with this "visual proof" and what occurs in the present day will begin to write a new story within your culture versus one that is solely rooted in the past.

Uncovering Other Centers of Influence to Help You

Advice doesn't just come from the Insightful Leader at the top of the organization. Others can be elevated to that role too who may be ready to help you – and they don't even have to be located in the C-Suite. By finding and understanding other centers of influence in your organization, you have the great potential to empower people to engage with those influencers so they can be approached for advice.

So who *are* these centers of influence?

You know them. There are a handful of them in every organization. It's those special individuals who know the ins-and-outs of certain challenges better than anybody. Everyone knows that Bob is the one to attack a particular issue while Roy is someone to see when you want to address another specific issue. It comes from building up a reputation for solutions when these scenarios arise.

They're the people you go to in order to ask questions, no matter what their title is. It's what makes them **De Facto Leaders**.

On the **Reality Chart**, one person is the one you'll always go to for answers. We'll call her Jane. On the **Organizational Chart**, there's the person who actually has designated responsibility for that area. We'll call him Fred.

Now, if Fred *really* wants to get things done, he doesn't need to necessarily give Jane the authority to do it. But he does need to tell everyone, including Jane, that if they have an issue, it would be a good idea to touch base with Jane to see what she thinks. Jane and the rest of the team need to be comfortable with that.

What if those De Facto Leaders don't have the capability or interest like you thought? What if they already have a full plate and don't have time to get their own job done as it is without having more added to it in the form of others asking them advice?

True, not everyone is able to engage and advise. Regardless of that fact, your environment must display that everyone has the right to ask questions and encourage them to do so.

When Advice Gives Way to Action

If you study any great military leader, you can see a pattern among the most successful ones. First, if there is time, they'll listen to multiple opinions and open the floor to others so they can provide a potential way forward. Then, at some point, the leader will realize that the time for collaborating, discussing and yes, arguing, is over. Now is the time for a decision to be made. The leader makes a choice and accepts full responsibility for that decision. Everyone needs to understand, however, that there are some decisions that have to be made without any group discussion. This does not change the leader's interest in soliciting opinions. It just means that the climate at that moment mandates that a decision be made.

How different is that really from the business world? Not as different as you think.

After all, being an Insightful Leader means both understanding how everyone else is thinking and the climate in which you are operating as well as being decisive on the next steps. All the while, as you're making that decision, you have to convey the role of each person in helping move it forward.

People will have questions. You as the Insightful Leader, along with De Facto Leaders, will have advice to share. The communication never really stops. Nor should it ever. This ideally breeds a culture where people can feel that they're being heard and their careers are being nurtured. A host of benefits, including greater employee satisfaction and retention, can rise to the surface.

Dan Gershenson
CEO
Caliber Brand Strategy + Content Marketing

As I was coming up in the advertising agency world as a Copywriter, my Creative Director took me aside one day and said, *"Dan, you're very good at what you do as a writer. If you want, you could do it for an awfully long time successfully. But if you want to get out from behind a desk and grow your career, you need to learn how to present your work with great polish to others, both internally to colleagues and externally to clients."*

In that moment, the advice he provided changed my career forever. He pushed me way outside of my comfort zone and pointed me toward a comedy improvisation class of all things to gain experience as a presenter. He didn't say, *"This is what I did to improve myself and this is what you should do too."*

In my case, as with others I've managed, the person you are potentially advising isn't aware of how to seize their potential fully, but when they are enlightened to the resources and tools to actually take that next step, they are inspired to learn more. Because in that moment, their leader is now their advisor and has taken the time to give some tips that may enhance their professional life.

I can't stress one key point enough, however – I've never worked well with micromanagers and I don't think a lot of people do. So it's critical that as you're advising, you have to give that individual some guidance, but you also have to recognize when it's time to get the hell out of the way. Let them forge their own path based on your words of wisdom because they need to feel like they're writing their own story rather than living someone else's life – no matter how successful you've been in a leadership role.

I'm a big sports fan and this advisory relationship versus leading reminds me of how a pro baseball team has its "farm" teams of talent to draft and develop. You can give them all the equipment and coaching in the world, but in the end, they've got to want to take the next step in their professional evolution (or not) through a strong commitment to doing so. **You can't make them want that.**

It's your job as an Insightful Leader to shine a light on the best avenues and options for their success based on your experience. It's very easy to get almost too comfortable at times wearing the "hat" of what you do best. I was there. Yet, when an Insightful Leader showed me how I could be something more, I was inspired by the possibility. The key is, even as their eyes are lighting up and they're touched that their leader – you – wants to be an advocate for their future, you still need to strike an important balance that sets expectations of what you will **and won't** do for them. Namely, rather than lead them to the exact point that worked for you, I find being in the advisory role gives emerging talent the comfort and confidence that the expertise they need is never far when they need it most. As both the person who has been advised and the person doing the advising, I have found advising to be one of the most gratifying experiences of my career.

TAKEAWAYS

❖ You want to be in a position where your opinions are requested, respected and acted on. This objective can be accomplished in a number of ways, including advising others. Not just leading alone.

❖ Determine if and how you want to get into the advice realm. Do you want to mentor, join an informal advisory group or join a formal Board?

❖ In each of these advisory roles, you need to set expectations, both on yourself as well as on those to whom you are giving the advice. How much time will you spend? How will your advice be acted upon?

EXERCISES

❖ Identify an organization with whom you are not
currently affiliated that should ask for your advice.

❖ Articulate three questions you would ask people in that
organization to understand the type of advice they seek

DECISION MATRIX QUESTIONS

❖ Do I have the time to offer my counsel to others?

❖ How will my counsel be used?

❖ If on a Board, will I be paid for providing this counsel?

❖ What can I learn from giving advice?

8

Being an Adaptive Leader

"I had limited tolerance for mediocrity, but I did not really understand that as a team, we could do more. I had to learn to respect the contributions of all, work with the full team as a whole and all of the members individually...to bring them to exceptional."

Aziz Asphahani, CEO, QuesTek Innovations

How many times have you heard a leader say, *"Why aren't they getting it? Why doesn't the team react to the directions or follow my orders?"*

Well, is the issue the leader or the team?

Individuals have their preferred styles of how they want to operate as well as how they want to be led.

In the same breath, **an individual's personal style as to how they want to be led can change dramatically depending on activities that are going on with them,** from their child being sick to a parent passing away. Also note that the team member as well as the team leader's style can change dependent on the "newness" of the situation as well as the perceived urgency of getting something done.

Furthermore, as Insightful Leaders, we also need to be able to honestly look in the mirror and understand what is going on in our own heads. And then, be able to adapt how we are leading to our personal circumstances as well.

When our team members are going through some kind of an emotional trauma, they may not be comfortable doing things "business as usual" and could need some help so that they aren't immersed in grief or other emotions. However, while sometimes they will overtly ask for help, more often...they won't.

That's when you, as an Insightful Leader, need to have a good enough understanding of the people you're responsible for as you aim to keep the momentum of business humming along.

That can sound a bit like this:

> *"I'm so sorry that this happened but we really need to get this out. I need you to do X, Y, Z on this. So are you able and comfortable with this? Can I just leave you to do this or do you need help?"*

You're adapting your style to what's going on in the person's head and in their life. Different times and situations call for a different kind of leadership. That's why an Insightful Leader practices **adaptive leadership**, such as:

➢ **Dealing with a person differently than you normally would due to unique circumstances**

➢ **Dealing with a person differently than the leadership style that you've portrayed to the team**

Why do we need to constantly adapt when we lead?

Let me give you an example to illustrate why these "microstyles" can be valuable.

I was working in a department where a meeting notice was put out on a particular topic. Fairly harmless, right?

After I ran into one of the senior people of the organization, it was clear to me that it wasn't going to be an easy meeting. The person who called the meeting was just the type to stand in your face and yell at you – a tone-deaf individual who would only transmit "this is my way to do things" messages and was never in receive mode.

As much as I tried to explain that this impending doom was coming in our meeting, my colleague didn't think that would happen.

I hoped she was right. But unfortunately, I was. That's exactly what happened. The person who called the meeting yelled and did not stop for the entire meeting. He pounded on the table. He was right and everyone was wrong.

I shouldn't have been that surprised. I was relatively new to the organization and everybody was saying to me, *"This is how this guy is. He never listens."* But then I had the opportunity to sit down with him for a one-on-one conversation. Want to know something remarkable? He really had some neat insights into what I wanted to do and where I wanted to go.

The only time I ever saw this person like that was in one-on-one meetings. When there were more than two people in the room, everything changed and he believed that he knew what was best.

My point is this:

You can have a different public persona from your private persona.

This may seem in conflict with the idea that a leader needs to be consistent in message. However, if you sufficiently explain to someone on your team that you may have a conversation with them one-on-one and you're not going to change what you're doing when in a group setting, but you may portray the case a little bit differently to the group in order to get the group motivated.

You need to be able to look at yourself in the mirror and say, "*This is who I am. Under these circumstances, I can do X and under these circumstances, I can do Y.*"

I met an Army General who once told me:

> "*Look, when I can, I encourage discussion. I encourage collaboration. But I'm also cognizant of the fact that I need people to act when it is time to act. There are going to be times when I say this is what we're going to do and when we're going to start doing it. I may take some input before that, but I'm going to tell you what we're going to do. It's not necessarily going to be that I don't want to build consensus. However, there are times when we just need to get over it and get on with it.*"

Situational awareness. It means fully understanding the *people* you're dealing with as well as the *situation* you're dealing with them in.

So – Which Leadership Style Is Yours?

There are many different styles of leadership, but for the most part, a leader will focus on one style and work through the positive and negative aspects of that specific style.

Some of the better-known examples include:

> ➢ **Dictator**

You take the hill. You have what you need to succeed. Now get on with it. I'll tell you what to do and when. If you deviate from that plan, it's going to result in real, most likely negative, consequences for you.

> ➢ **Follow Me**

We're going to take that hill. I will lead the way. Keep up with me and let's go.

> ➢ **Collaborator**

We are going to take that hill. I am right next to you. Let's go and let me know if you need me to define the steps.

> ➢ **Remote**

Your job is to take the hill. I will be here and available for advice and counsel to you. I'll also be here for the other leaders who are taking their own hills. Ask for help if and as you need it.

There are, of course, a myriad of other styles. However, what is rarely talked about is **the need for the leader to be adaptive when dealing with the members of his or her team.**

While there needs to be a public persona of the leader, it is also necessary to understand *the needs of each member of one's team.* There are very few teams where each member responds to direction in the same way.

"You learn as much from being mentored as from mentoring."

Marie Marcenac, Global VP, Sales and Marketing, Carus Group, Inc.

The Insightful Leader knows that she needs to understand each member of the team, as well as herself, so that she can communicate to and with that member appropriately.

Does it take more time? Perhaps. Is the outcome better? Usually.

Edward Holland
President and CEO
M. Holland Company

After taking his last finals exam in college, getting married and going on his honeymoon, Ed Holland promptly went to work for his father's firm, M. Holland Company, in 1976. At the time, he was the company's 6th employee. Today, as President and CEO, Ed oversees an organization of over $1 billion in revenue that has grown to become "The Gold Standard" in resin distribution, with 182 employees working in the northern suburbs of Chicago, 50 in Mexico and 16 in Puerto Rico. He is responsible for protecting and advancing a company culture that is focused on attracting the very best talent in the industry.

One of my jobs as leader of this company is not only to get the right people on the bus but also to get the right people *in the right seats on that bus.* If you have someone who is not in an ideal position where they can use their strengths and talents, you're injuring the organization, wasting assets, creating conflict and allowing for a climate to take place in which there is a lack of job enjoyment. None of those are good.

It reminds me of a story. Years ago, my tennis partner was the late, great film critic Gene Siskel. We played in a number of community tournaments and although we weren't always very good, we were able to reach the Finals of one tournament in Michigan by beating some good people. However, now we were about to play against two doctors who were very active tennis players. If we played them 100 times, we'd probably lose 99. There was room for improvement.

So as Gene took a tennis lesson in the city, I went to a high school tennis coach for a lesson. After seeing me hit balls for five minutes, he said, *"I think I've figured out your game. Your forehand is very strong. Your net game is good. Your backhand is adequate. So, for the next hour, we're going to only focus on your forehand."* I was surprised by this response and asked him why we'd only work on what was already a strength of mine anyway.

He said, *"Well, we can work on your backhand in the next hour and get you to a place where maybe that's good and you can keep points alive. But you won't hit too many winners and you'll probably just prolong points that you'll eventually lose. On the other hand, if we work on your forehand, we can turn that into a devastating weapon that punishes your opponents and wins you points."*

Lo and behold, after taking that coach's advice, Gene and I went on to win the tournament in Michigan.

I didn't really think about that story until October 2003. My brother had just left the company and I made four moves on the organizational chart that, if you went by that org chart alone, would be seen as demotions. So when I gave a "State of the Company" speech to our employees two months later, there already was a lot of negative energy permeating through the room.

I decided to tell my story of my tennis lesson and winning the tournament. I told the employees, *"What we're doing by these moves is putting people in jobs where they can use their forehand."* All of the sudden, those people who had seen themselves as demoted were now empowered. They realized they could now "use their forehand" to succeed. The negative energy sucked out of the room that day and stayed out. In fact, these days, the colloquialism in the company is *"that's his forehand"* or *"that's not his forehand."*

I believe that's part of leadership – gaining the trust of your people to create the behaviors and actions you'd like. Call it "Winning hearts and minds." If you win hearts and minds the actions follow. If you don't win hearts and minds, everything else is pushing a rock uphill.

TAKEAWAYS

❖ What are the differences in required communication for people with different leadership styles?

❖ Is there a set of questions you can use to determine individual needs?

❖ How does one communicate to the entire team that the leader is genuine, even though they may have different styles in private?

❖ What are types you're comfortable with on your team and what happens when you encounter a new one?

❖ How do you deal with someone who doesn't want to be or can't be led?

EXERCISES

❖ With a similar goal, describe how you would deal with someone who needs each of these styles:

    Follow Me
    Collaborator
    Remote

❖ Now, do the same thing as a team member as opposed to a team leader. Describe how you would respond to being led by each type.

DECISION MATRIX QUESTIONS

❖ How do you decide on public persona?

❖ How do you determine which styles to work with on your team?

9

Evolution of a Leadership Decision Matrix

"Do the best you can. One needs to understand that you can't always control the outcome, but things will work out."

Bob Hughes
Colonel, US Army (Ret.) and
Clinical Assistant Professor Kellogg School of Management

At the end of each chapter, you may recall we had a series of questions related to that chapter's subject matter. If we now select at least one of those questions per chapter, we can create a **Decision Matrix to help you customize a path forward that will ultimately enhance how you lead today as well as tomorrow.**

The purpose for taking these Decision Matrix questions into consideration is to give you a sense of the process when I answer these questions for myself. Therefore, the questions I've selected and subsequent answers may not be the same ones you will have. However, by answering the questions that these chapters have raised for me, my hope is to illustrate the process for you that I've followed in attacking these decision points throughout my career.

What are the areas in which people seek my counsel?

Depending on the circumstances, you may find yourself as: *The Leader, The De Facto Leader, The Advisor.*

Let's face it. When we're asked to give advice to others, it feels good – so good, in fact, that we just give it, give it and give it some more. However, rarely do we ever stop to realize why these people come to us for advice in the first place.

What can we do, as leaders, De Facto Leaders or advisors to get a better understanding of what it is that people really come to us for so that the next time someone comes to us, we can recognize it and be that much more prepared?

My answer is there are two ways to do that – both of which demand a great amount of preparation:

For one, you never know who's going to knock on your door for advice, but before you start responding to that person's question, you might say, *"Let me just ask you a couple of questions before we start. I'd like a better* **understanding of the context for you asking this question."**

> *"Are you asking this question out of general interest and don't have specific responsibility for taking action as a result of this conversation? Or are you asking because you're leading a team with a specific responsibility and you're trying to make a decision about the team's direction? Or are you a member of a team, where you've been asked to provide some input into the direction that the team is going?"*

By asking these questions and getting a level set, you can then understand the context, which is crucial.

Secondly, **find parallel situations in your past experience** that can address the question before you today – it doesn't have to overlap perfectly, but it should provide some similarities for the sake of clarity.

> *"You know, while we were facing a slightly different issue back then versus what you're facing today, there are still many similarities. Here's the way we went about seeking the answers in the context that you're in, in order to figure our way across a difficult challenge."*

Do I understand my short-term and long-term leadership objectives?

Based on this question, you may in turn ask,

> *"How do I define short-term and how do I define long-term? Is it the one-year and the five-year plan? Is it the five-year and the 10-year plan? Is it the full career plan?"*

As a leader, you likely have many years of experience to enable you to hold that role, but also think about different jobs that you've held along the way and consider the positions you've held.

If you break it down to short- and long-term objectives within the current position, if your title is Manager of Budgets and Planning for example, do you understand what your short-term objectives are within that? Do you understand your long-term objective to continue to be the Manager of Budgets and Planning, but instead of viewing it through the lens of just for your organization, could you be that manager for five or six organizations? Do you know if that is possible?

From there, do you want to stay in the silo of that role or do you want to escape from it? For example, Manager of Budgets and Planning may imply a little bit of work around finance. Do you also want to have responsibility for strategy beyond the financial work? Do you want to have responsibility for people planning beyond the strategy, financial and budgeting work? Do you want to have greater responsibilities within a narrow organization or do you want to broaden that out to more organizations?

Within your organization, if you know what you want to do, are you going to need to leave at some point because that business isn't big enough to really get you the opportunity you want?

When I'm working with companies in planning, the first question is: *"How do you define long-term?"* As we set up a plan, long-term could mean next week or even every hour, especially when you have to make amazingly difficult decisions. Some leaders can't think beyond next week. It's about understanding what the horizon is and then understanding that you still occasionally need to lift your head up to try to look a little bit beyond the horizon.

Do we understand what we are responsible for?
Do we understand how we fit in the organization?
Do I understand the individuals on my team?
Do I understand the intra- and inter-team dynamics?

Managers tend to define things as, *"Here's the set of things we need to do and here's the prescriptive order for how to get it done."* However, when you become a leader, it's more along the lines of, *"Here's what our goal set is and we now have to figure out as a team how we're going to get it done."*

It's about understanding the entirety of what the organization is doing and how your team fits. The intra-team dynamic involves identifying who's responsible for the goal, who else knows something about it and who thinks they know a lot about it even though they clearly don't.

That's why we want to make sure we understand everything that's going on before we start asking (and answering) a flurry of questions. What are the skill sets in front of us and where does each individual's strength lie? How does each individual wish to grow? How can our team grow within the organization and gain greater visibility, recognition, etc. as a key contributor on projects? As an

Insightful Leader, you're not only looking for how you personally can help team members with their individual goals but also where else you can send them in the organization outside of their team in order to achieve their short-term and long-term goals.

The Insightful Leader needs to have the perspective and vision to understand the individual, understand how that individual fits within the team and finally, how the team fits within the organization. Along the way, it's vital that you help to chart a course at each segment in a collaborative yet decisive manner that encourages the individual and team to take ownership of the goals you've mutually agreed upon.

Are there people/functional disciplines in my organization I need to learn how to communicate with?

Are you assuming that as a leader, you are supposed to know the answers to all the questions? There may be types of questions that you're not comfortable asking because they're specific to things that you don't know anything about.

With this in mind, are there people in functional disciplines that you need to learn how to communicate with? And are you at ease with asking intelligent questions to people in areas other than what your expertise is?

It's about getting yourself to a point of being able to engage in conversation with these folks and helping them think – because that's really why you ask questions: to help them think.

When you think about hiring, I don't recommend you try to hire people who are *just like you*. Instead, try to hire people who have different world views or come from different places so that there are other perspectives being brought to the dialogue.

You also need to constantly work on understanding how to talk to these different people. Take the generational differences, for example. If you're a Baby Boomer, how do you talk to Gen X, Gen Y and Millennials?

How do you talk about work with and to them? You may have a certain way of expressing yourself to others, but you also need to constantly listen and watch for feedback, whether it's body language, specific questions you're asked, etc. to make sure that you're getting through to the people.

So, there are always people you need to learn how to communicate with and it's not as if you're going to check a box and say, "Okay. Today I've learned how to talk to a Millennial. I'm done. I can move on now." Because everybody is a different individual. It's about being willing to understand each individual that you're dealing with in your organization.

You need to constantly build your pile of things that you need to understand about every person that you're communicating with.

What are the takeaways from coming in second or last? Do we believe we can dust ourselves off easily and get on with life? Why or why not?

The word "easily" is so important to the second question. Do we believe we can dust ourselves off and get on with life? Yes. Do we believe we can dust ourselves off *easily*? No. You will never win 100% of the time, but you shouldn't like losing. At the same time, when you lose something, know that if you don't dust yourself off and get on with life, that's not good. As best you can, you've got to get over it and get on with it.

Therefore, do you have a mechanism where you can **learn from what happened**? As an analogy, let's say you are in a quarter mile race and you lose. Did you lose the race because you were literally not as fast as the person that you were running against? Did you lose the race because the other person just had a much quicker start? Did you lose because you were wearing the wrong shoes for the track? Did you lose the race because you really weren't in shape to run a quarter mile race in the first place?

As you go through these questions and answer them one by one, you may learn quite a bit about the reasons for why you lost the race. Not as fast as that competitor who won? You can try to work on that and train harder. Not in good enough shape to finish the race? There are a lot of things you can do about that too. Didn't have the right shoes? Didn't have as fast of a start? There are also things that can be potentially improved upon with time and focus. You may also review pictures of different portions of the race to see where you fell behind.

Now let's apply this same kind of post-mortem work to the business world.

Why is it that you didn't win that proposal?

- ➤ Were you overpriced?
- ➤ Was the time that you suggested to do the deal too long?
- ➤ Did you really understand what it was that the customer was asking for?
- ➤ Did the customer say, "*I want to talk about X,*" but you went in and talked to him about Y and Z without ever fully talking to him about X?

Asking all of these questions and more requires the capability to do a post-mortem in an honest and forthright manner. Doing so determines if we can dust ourselves off and get on with life.

Can you dust yourselves off and get on with life? Do you have the emotional wherewithal to look at what went wrong? Do you have the emotional wherewithal to say, "*OK, what do I need to change?*"

If you are the team leader, you may need to honestly ask,

> *"Am I the right person to lead this effort?"* It's also about looking at the team and asking, *"Are we the right team to attack this problem? Or do we have a gaping hole in our team? Do we have somebody on the team that's really not up to snuff? It's all of these kinds of analytical pieces and then what are we going to do the next time?"*

To be clear, the post-mortem is never a blame game session. It's not where you might say, *"Well, Jim just didn't pull his weight and that's why we lost."* Break away from the finger-pointing and speak to what you as a team can do better next time to improve and increase your odds of winning next time.

The reality is, in business, you don't always know why you lost. You can ask questions to learn why and establish relationships with the people you are attempting to win business with by receiving honest feedback from them. Just make sure you do your post-mortem within a couple days of the loss while all the factors are still fresh in people's minds. Don't pretend it didn't happen or run from it. Face it head on, learn from what went wrong, dust yourself off and as a result, you're more likely to become a better version of yourself, the Insightful Leader, the next time.

Do I understand the generational differences apparent and inherent in the teams that I am leading?

The **speed of life** is different depending on where you are in the moment. Our speed of life is dictated by the device formerly known as a cell phone (I actually wish I had come up with that line myself!). Think about your instantaneous access to everything from this device. If you were to go on a safari in Africa tomorrow, I would wager there are still places that don't have good cell phone coverage, just like there are probably still places in the United States that don't have good cell phone coverage. In these more remote areas, they really don't have the speed of data that you're used to, so you can't get the access.

Knowing this, can we then expect that response times will be the same? Of course not. It's no different than if we were dealing with somebody who still carries a flip phone and doesn't have access to all of this information flow that the rest of us commonly have.

When we speak to generational differences, we have to well define each other's expectations in terms of response times.

You may decide that, for one hour every day, you're going to turn everything off, including your cell phone. What if someone needs you during that time period? Well, those people need to understand that there are times during the day when you're going to be turned "off." You can't respond to them instantaneously.

So each party needs to understand enough about each other as far as how responses are handled.

In the very old days, you would send a letter and after several days, you might get a letter back from that recipient. Then you moved to sending a fax. Then you began to be able to leave a voicemail. And today, you send a text.

The point being, the generational differences have been such that if you were to send something through the mail, obviously there would be an expectation of the pace at which the communication moves. Conversely, in today's age, if you're leaving a voicemail for someone and you know that person's phone is always on, you have a much different set of expectations about the response time, right? Email and texting may be even more accelerated expectations.

We have a different subconscious expectation with regard to which people we're sending the messages to. And because of how (and when) you've grown up and the industries you may have worked in, you can have a different set of expectations. In fact, if you sent the same message to two people, you shouldn't be shocked to discover a different level of response based on their generation and experience.

It's important that you, the Insightful Leader, not paint with such a broad and generalized brush to assume that one generation falls into the same response time bucket. That said, if you're dealing with a group of people that are in their 40s or 30s or 20s, you may form an expectation based on how these groups respond – that's OK as long as you are in a state of continuously evolving that expectation based on responses. Then, as you continue to deal with them, the picture becomes all the more clearer and if you have to modify your expectations, so be it.

So while there is a generational aspect to understanding teams, there is also an individual aspect in getting to know each person on the team. What is their perspective on the speed of life?

When you're building that relationship, getting closer to them, drilling down from generational to team to individual, what makes this individual tick? Having a constant communication with them, puts you, in turn, into a position of being an Insightful Leader.

What can I learn from giving advice?

Actually, start from a related question to this by asking yourself: **How do I give advice?**

If you give **advice by direction**, then you probably can't learn that much.

If you give **advice by questioning**, you may still have an opinion, but you're going to seek to understand at the same time. You're going to help or attempt to push the discussion into a place where questions are asked like, *"Have you thought about that?"* In the process, we'll arrive at things that we're unlikely to have seen or heard before.

What can you learn from giving advice? For one, know that there is rarely, if ever, one correct answer. By asking questions, you're going to come upon new, fresh ideas that you hadn't really considered.

With this in mind, when leading a business and creating an environment for team success, you have to embrace the opportunities that come with bringing aboard new employees with diverse perspectives. As a result, you're bound to hear (or say yourself), *"Wow, I never would have thought of that!"*

You can't get there by giving advice by direction and instructing people to follow a specific path. You're just not going to learn a lot from that. However, if you have a goal that you want to increase your business by 50%, for example, what are the milestones we need to consider? What are the metrics of success along the way? Some of those metrics may be ones we haven't thought of.

So through the course of a more open-ended discussion rooted in a series of questions, you as an Insightful Leader can open your eyes up more to new possibilities based on other peoples' experiences. Not just your own.

This is how you can learn from giving advice – the *way* you actually give advice can make all the difference in whether you discover new frontiers for your business.

How do you determine which styles to work with on your team?

Part of this question comes down to asking: *What is your team charged with doing?*

Let's say you are charged with developing a brand-new technology and taking that to market. You don't particularly like working with the kind of people who show up in the morning, go into their office, close the door, sit the whole day pounding on their computer and then get up to leave at night but never say goodbye to anybody. In fact, you may say, *"Boy, I just don't want to work with introverted people on a project like this."* But wait just a minute. Take a step back. Can you honestly accomplish your goals set forth for the team <u>without</u> that person if they're that important but have a personality that's very different?

If you can't accomplish those goals, the next logical question is: What do you need to do even though you may not enjoy working with that person? What do you need to do to encourage the rest of the team to do in regard to how you're going to work with this person?

Because if you can't get the ball over the goal line without that person, then saying you're <u>never</u> going to work with an introvert means your odds of success are significantly diminished.

In addition to deciding which styles you need to have on your team, the other piece of this equation is deciding **how to coach your team members to reach a level where they become high functioning contributors.**

For example, when you ask general questions in staff meetings such as, *"What do you think about that,"* you don't want to hear a team member say, *"This is outside of my expertise and therefore I have no opinion."*

To which I would pull that person aside later and say, *"Look, some things may very well be outside of your expertise, but if you've got an opinion, you're required to participate in the discussion. You may be an introvert and refuse to participate, but I'm going to tell you that I think you've got something to contribute –even if you think you don't. So be ready. I'm going to be asking you a variety of questions because I believe you have much to offer this group and discussion."*

This doesn't mean the Insightful Leader tries to transform an introvert into an extrovert. It means you need to help this individual develop into more of the real team player than they ever thought they'd become.

TAKEAWAYS

❖ Don't just finish the book and put it on the shelf. When you are facing difficult issues, build your own process of asking and answering questions regarding your decision.

❖ Learn from the answers to your own questions so that each time you face an issue you can distill what you already know, you can understand what part of the situation is the same and what is different from the last time you addressed the issue, and you can focus your energy and time on what is different.

❖ Build a process for delineating between what is NICE TO KNOW when facing an issue and what you NEED TO KNOW and then don't make the decision until the NEED TO KNOW questions have been answered.

10

Building and Strengthening Your Personal Advisory Board

"If you don't listen, you won't get feedback. You need to understand your personal advisory board and what you are being held accountable for."

Gail Meneley, Partner, Shields Meneley Partners

We've talked about the journey of leading to advising. Ironically, here at the end of that journey, we're going to go back to the beginning to introduce a more personal concept.

In a business, you may enlist a Six Sigma mentality to improve upon your direction: Define, Measure, Analyze, Improve and Control.

In your personal life, you may have a different set of objectives and challenges, but the principle of defining your direction, measuring your progress, analyzing, making adjustments to improve, etc. is just as relevant.

With this in mind, wouldn't it be wise to have a group of advisors working with you on a more personal level, just like a traditional board within a company?

For all of the discussion regarding boards, most of the time we're focused on the formal structure supporting the business. While we believe that you as the Insightful Leader should push to have an active and engaged board for your business, whether fiduciary or advisory, you should also have a **Personal Advisory Board** to help provide advice and counsel on your *personal journey*.

If you have a friend or family member whom you are marching on this path with, whether that's a brother, a mother or a college roommate, you have someone who understands where you've been and where you want to go from here.

Does an advisory board operate exactly like a fiduciary board in a business setting? No. An advisory board is a board that gives you advice and counsel, but they aren't involved in your day-to-day operations. Rarely are they given the right to make *binding* decisions as opposed to a fiduciary board that does the review of the CEO and can come in and tell an executive, *"you're gone."*

If you're going to set objectives for your personal life as well as your career, you not only need to set expectations for yourself but also work with other people close to you to define and refine those expectations. That's only going to help you get to where you want to go quicker.

Let's meet some examples of these informal – yet extremely important – advisors on your Personal Advisory Board.

Who Is On Your Personal Advisory Board?

Start by thinking about your goals for this board and recognize that some members will have more expertise to help in a specialized area than others based on their background.

For example, you may need professional advice and counsel on writing a will or understanding your financial plan. Your **personal attorney** may help with the will while management of your financial assets could require a **financial planner** you're comfortable with. In addition to their skill set, you have the kind of close relationship in which you trust that they are working with you to help you achieve your goals.

If you're a particularly spiritual person and require guidance, you can turn to a spiritual leader such as your **Rabbi, Pastor, Imam** or a close friend you're comfortable talking to.

Let's not forget about one of the most crucial of confidantes: Your **life partner or spouse**. They know everything there is to know about you, including your innermost dreams, thoughts and fears.

For so many leaders, **friends and family** are going to play a big role too. One of my favorite toasts at gatherings sounds like this: *This toast is to my friends who are my family and my family who are my friends.* That's the way I feel about my brother, a person I always talk to when I'm making an important decision. It's also the way I feel about a few classmates I went to school with from Northwestern whenever we talk about where we're headed in our lives and how we'll get to the next magical destination. When any of these trusted people answer a question, they're doing so because of what they feel is the best possible outcome for you.

Are all your answers going to come from this group exclusively and directly? Surprisingly, no. When you bring a Personal Advisory Board together, you'll find that there are **concentric circles of influence** at work. What I mean by that is that there are people who will sit at the table with you, but then there will be people that they know that you haven't been fortunate enough to meet yet. These circles of influence can have an impact by association if those closest to you in turn have a close relationship with those who have provided insight to them that you can use.

Importing your skills into a new organization is also why a Personal Advisory Board has such merit. Think about all the things that could pull at you at one time as a leader. This type of board will help you work through the issues associated with an ever-changing landscape. Let's say the senior leadership of a family business is transitioning out – in that event, they need to bring in an outside board composed of people who can advise them. But they could decide to bring in both a formal board for advice on operational matters and a personal board for counsel on matters impacting family relationships.

Accountability Is Key: It's Not Advice For The Sake Of It.

If a person is going to come to you for the next several years to provide advice and counsel, you have to chart a course that involves goal setting and tracking accomplishments.

For example, you and your Personal Advisory Board agree on certain things that you are going to achieve six months from now. Six months later during one of your meetings, you reveal that you haven't made very much progress on those achievements and want more input from the board.

Wait a minute. You said those goals were important to you. Why haven't you done anything about it? What are you going to do about it? If you said you wanted to serve on a non-profit board, have you looked into the kinds of organizations that need someone like you? Do you know anybody on those boards? See, even a Personal Advisory Board member can push back. Because when you're comfortable stating your objectives and having key checkpoints to track progress, it's a discussion with purpose and accountability built in. If you don't have that, you risk one of those people saying, *"You're asking for my advice but this is the third time I've checked and you still haven't done anything on that? You're wasting my time."*

This does not mean that you have to agree and do everything the board recommends, but you must be ready to say why you can't do or won't do what they're recommending.

Here Comes The Truth. Can You Handle It?

Admittedly, one of the tougher parts of implementing a Personal Advisory Board consisting of the people you're closest to is that you can't build a Fan Club. If someone is your advisor and vice versa, there has to be a degree of **independence.** They need to be able to tell you when you're full of BS. In return, you need to be able to express your unvarnished opinion and truth to them as you see it.

If it gets to the point where they're not taking your advice (or you taking theirs), you should obviously aim to preserve the friendship but in the same breath, look to someone else for advice who can tell you what you *need* to hear, not what you *want* to hear.

My wife and I talk about things all the time, so when I decided I was leaving a company I'd been employed with for many years, she asked, "*What's taken you so long? You've been miserable. Leave!*" I then asked others in my personal circle for their unvarnished opinion: Should I stick around or take off? From an external perception, what do you think? If my business card had a different title, what would that mean? How will I support myself if I walk out the door?

John Tinghitella
President / Owner
RV Designer

John had already spent the majority of his career with companies in the marine and pleasure boat RV markets when he had an epiphany: He needed to get out of a corporate world that was continuously stifling his creativity. That's when he decided to become an owner and purchase the business of RV Designer, a leading supplier in the U.S. of products to the RV after market. Since 2010, he has been focused on delivering sustained, healthy growth to the company while forming a world-class team.

When you own or run a business, part of the problem is that you don't have a boss! Now, perhaps a certain entrepreneurial spirit doesn't want a boss, but to some extent I need one – not necessarily someone to tell me what to do, but someone I can be held accountable to.

I'm also always looking for a community of like-minded people. The sense of community I get from my current personal advisory board is a lot of shared experiences. Yes, I have a depth of experience I can provide them, but I also pick up many pieces of insight from them as well. They have helped me work through some things that I'm not bad at but I'm not great at either.

For example, I'm very good at *running* a business but I don't consider myself the best at *owning* a business. I believe I actually perform many things I'm supposed to do as an owner – but can I tell you something? *I just don't like it.* I wish I liked it but I don't! I suppose, with a lot of skin in the game, I'm more conservative than I thought I was. I'm learning to manage that. I'm hoping to get good at it. This much I do know: The personal advisory board I have helps me be better at it.

Case in point: Cash crunches bother the living hell out of me but if you talk to any of the people on my personal advisory board, you'd think it's as natural as breathing. So, I'm learning to gain the fortitude to get through those challenges as a small business owner. That's the primary aspect that's surprised me the most – the psychological impact of being an owner, which is mainly about the money aspect. However, with a personal advisory board that brings me greater perspective while holding me accountable, I don't believe there's any surprise as the result of being an owner that I can't handle.

The work toward becoming an Insightful Leader makes for a purposeful journey and one you need not go on alone. Select wisely to ensure the right people are coming with.

TAKEAWAYS

❖ It's never too early to start building the list of issues you want to have outside counsel on.

❖ Understand that the list will be modified over time.

❖ As the list changes, the people to whom you will go for counsel may change as well.

❖ Be honest on what you have or have not accomplished and why.

EXERCISES

❖ Define the purpose for your initial Personal Advisory Board, that is, what is the list of three to five issues that you want all or some of these advisors to help you address.

❖ Define your three to five, time-bound goals that you want you want your advisors' counsel on.

❖ Begin to define your process for evaluation of existing goals and issues.

DECISION MATRIX QUESTIONS

❖ When is it appropriate to add or delete someone from my board?

❖ When is it appropriate to bring the board in for consultation?

A Final Word

The irony of having a final word on *Becoming An Insightful Leader* is that, at its best, there is no final word. It is a goal. It is by no means an endpoint. Your journey from here will be an ongoing one in which you never truly stop learning as long as you have the courage to continually ask good questions of others and of yourself.

Take a moment to reflect on that. Rather than being one more leader who settles into the status quo, you have made the incredible commitment to evolve your leadership style based on the environment that surrounds you. It is an approach that I believe will not only serve you well, but also serve your organization and clients very well too.

As you go forward, I hope you will refer back to this book as a reference guide for the steps and checkpoints you're sure to experience.

May your path to *Becoming An Insightful Leader* be as fulfilling, exciting and meaningful as mine has been.

Acknowledgements

Throughout this book, I have spoken about the journey towards being and becoming an Insightful Leader. While the leadership journey is a continuous one, the process of writing a book does, eventually, come to an end. So, before I put down the pen – or more appropriately, save this last section on the laptop – I have to thank many people who have provided guidance along the way.

Before I started, I had a vague notion about what it would take to write a book. I am fortunate to have worked with two people though the last year who have helped me to focus and refine the work that I've been doing.

Sarah Victory of the Victory Company helped guide me through the process of determining the broad focus of the book. Sarah helped me to identify and articulate what an Insightful Leader is and we were off to the races. Dan Gershenson of Caliber Brand Strategy + Content Marketing has helped me to focus the message by continuing to question, refine and edit as we have moved through the later stages of the writing process. Both Sarah and Dan deserve much of the credit for helping me to bring this project over the finish line. THANK YOU.

Throughout the book, I have shared stories and quotations from a number of people. While a few of these were quotes picked up through the public media, I was fortunate to have had the opportunity to spend time personally interviewing over 50 business leaders during the course of writing the book. I have included a list of those interviewed at the end of this section. It should be noted that while some did not make it into these pages, all of their thoughts and concepts helped guide me and will serve as the basis of blogs and articles to come.

As I stated in the introduction, my perspectives on leadership were formed by observation of many whom I had the honor of working for, collaborating with and generally learning from throughout the years. While this list is long and continues to grow, three individuals in particular stand out.

I worked at Motorola during the time when Chris Galvin was Chairman. One of the key lessons that I learned from Chris was that everyone had something to offer and, in order to get the most out of each person, a fundamental level of respect needed to be offered to them. Chris embodied this then and continues to today.

I am a proud Alumnus of Northwestern University's Kellogg School of Management. While I was there, I was fortunate to meet Pete Henderson and Ed Wilson. Both of these individuals had the title of Dean. And both of them talked and walked a commitment to continued growth and to seeking constant improvement and excellence. I am happy to say that over the years, I have continued to learn about leadership from them and still consider them to be close friends.

Speaking of Kellogg, my co-conspirators from the Class of '80 continue to inspire me. Some of you have become treasured friends whose advice and counsel I value deeply. We have taken many paths and unfortunately, some of the crew are no longer with us. That said, over the last couple of years, Kellogg has articulated a number of themes. One spoke about the notion of *"Success to Significance."* We moved to the notion of *"Think Bravely"* and today work to *"Inspire Growth."* As I look at my classmates and those whom I have gotten to know who came before and followed us, I think that these taglines have served to both inform and guide us. You have all provided me with inspiration throughout this process.

My friends from Haverford also continue to inspire me. In particular, Tom Donnelly, my track coach, and three of my classmates, David Hackett, Tom Gerlach and Chris Jones all serve as role models for a variety of elements of striving for improvement.

My extended family, especially my sons Michael and Adam, provides critical feedback and encouragement. I am incredibly proud of who you are, welcome your questioning and insights and look forward to continuing to engage on the next steps of the journey.

And finally, thank you, thank you, thank you to my wife, Diana Cohen. You have provided crucial feedback and insightful guidance to me in my career as well as during the writing of this book.

Again, thank you to all and now, ONWARD.

Interview List

Lory	Aaron	Great America Finance
Susan	Aaron	Chaddick Institute, DePaul University
Aziz	Asphahani	Questek Innovations
Yulia	Austin	Carus Group
Stuart	Baum	Larger Pond Marketing
Bruce	Breitzman	Spartan Metals
David	Brown	ALP Lighting
Sue	Buchanan	Carus Group
Inga	Carus	Carus Group
Erv	Chambliss	Union College
Ted	Christian	Umoja
Karen	Demorest	Youth Job Center
Matt	Feldman	Federal Home Loan Bank, Chicago
Marc	Fern	M. Holland Company
Joe	Flanagan	Acquirent
Jim	Flanagan	Nuance Solutions
Michael	Folz	Balasa Dinverno Foltz
Jim	Ford	Trendway Corporation
Taylor	Gaines	T and T Digital Media
Steve	Gaither	JB Chicago
Jay	Goltz	Jayson Home/Artist Frame Services
Pedro	Guerrero	Guerrero
Steve	Haggerty	Haggerty Consulting
Kaili	Harding	Schaumburg Business Association
Carlos	Hevia	Carus Group
Tom	Hodgman	NatureVest, The Nature Conservancy
Ed	Holland	M. Holland Company
Glenn	Horton	Horton Insurance
Bob	Hughes	Kellogg School of Management
Eric	Jaffe	Total Insurance
Monique	Jones	Evanston Community Foundation
Ian	Kieninger	Avant Communications
Tom	Kinder	Plante Moran
Kevin	Kinsella	Vistage International
Julie	Koelzer	Tenant Advisors, Inc
Helen	Levinson	Indigo Interactive
Drew	Lydecker	Avant Communications
Marie	Marcenac	Carus Group
Pat	McKune	M. Holland Company
Gail	Meneley	Shields Meneley Partners
Kevin	Mott	Edward Jones
Dev	Mukherjee	DePaul University
Richard	Nathan	RTC
Mike	Petersen	Petersen Aluminum
Michael	Rosengarden	Autohaus on Edens
Bruce	Rubin	BHR Global Associates
Reggie	Rush	DivIHN Integration Inc
Staci	Scharadin	Diamond Wealth Management
Steven	Schroeder	creative werks
Mark	Shapiro	Vistage International
Helena	Stelnicki	Stelnicki Advisors
Martin	Swarbrick	Pro Link Investment, Inc
John	Tinghitella	RV Designer Collection
Debra	Wold	Corporate Cup Celebrity Challenge

About The Author

 David Spitulnik is a successful executive with over 35 years' experience in both large technology companies and in consulting to and leadership of mid-market, closely held and family owned businesses across a variety of industries. As Managing Partner of Spitulnik Advisors, David is an Executive Coach and works with organizations to develop and implement strategies that drive transformation, growth, diversification, operating efficiency, and value creation. He is a catalyst for change with the ability to drive ideas from concept through successful execution. David is a leader and member of motivated, high performance teams who builds strong relationships with customers, business leaders, team members and government officials. He has broad governance experience on not-for-profit, corporate and advisory boards in the United States and internationally. David graduated from Haverford College with a B.A. in Economics and received his MBA from the Kellogg School of Management at Northwestern University.

To stay up to date on what David is thinking and writing, follow him on LinkedIn.

LinkedIn: davidspitulnik

CPSIA information can be obtained
at www.ICGtesting.com
Printed in the USA
JSHW021028150919
1410JS00008BA/23